D1603596

No Weeping Widow Here
My True Story

Victoria Benoit

Extraordinary Outcomes Publishing, LLC
Phoenix, Arizona

ExtraordinaryOutcomesPublishing.com

No Weeping Widow Here
My True Story

Copyright © 2023 by Victoria Benoit

Extraordinary Outcomes
PUBLISHING, LLC

ExtraordinaryOutcomesPublishing.com
Phoenix, Arizona

The events and experiences expressed herein reflect the author's faithful recollection of events. Dialogue has been re-created from memory. Some names, identities, and circumstances have been changed to protect the privacy of those involved. Many people generously allowed their names to be included.

Contributors:
Managing Editor: Paula Hofmeister
Cover Design & Book Layout: Betsy McGrew
Portrait Photograph: Glenn Mire
All other photos are the property of the author.

Printed in the United States of America
Library of Congress Cataloging-in-Publication Data
Paperback ISBN 978-0-9838567-4-0
eBook ISBN 978-0-9838567-5-7

No Weeping Widow Here™, *What Would Love Do Right Now? A Guide to Living an Extraordinary Life*™, *Inquiry to Resolution Process*™, *Three Magical Words for a Magical Life*™, *Conversations with the Fairy Realm*™, and *Adventures with the Fairy Realm*™ are trademarks of Victoria Benoit.

This book is dedicated to
my Beloved Bernie
who liberated his soul from his physical body
on November 27, 2017.

Thank you for ten wonderful years and all of the ways
you contributed your wisdom to my life and our happiness together.

Dearest Lyndis~
May this book enspire
you to open your heart
even more!
You are loved!
Victoria

Contents

Prologue

Our last weekend together began on Friday, November 24, 2017, when my Beloved Bernie told me, *"After tonight, honey, we'll have two more nights together."* Wow, how could he know? I completely dedicated the next three days to him—to us.

Bernie had been on oxygen constantly for a month. Now, the tumors in his lungs were so huge he could only breathe by sitting up in bed and leaning forward. Even though he had lost over 100 pounds, his body still looked beautiful to me. Wanting to be as close to him as possible, I embraced him from behind, holding him for hours. I read to him from an uplifting spiritual book he enjoyed, massaged his back, and made sure he had enough water. Throughout the weekend, I showed him how much he meant to me by looking into his soulful blue-green eyes and giving him a big smile of love, honor, and dignity. When he returned my smile, I felt washed in his love. These final days were tender, loving, and bittersweet.

Monday morning Bernie was restless and agitated, I thought he might be in pain. I gave him hourly doses of his oral medications to ease his breathing and reduce any discomfort. It settled him down considerably—I hoped I wasn't giving him too much. At one point, I remembered what he had said about us only having two more nights together, so I knew—today was the day.

I again held him close as he fought for every breath. All day, we listened to the inspirational sounds of spiritual music, filling the whole room with a sense of peace, calm, and sacredness.

His eldest son came over at 3:30. Fifteen minutes later, Bernie pulled off his oxygen mask. I suggested that his transition might be easier if he had some oxygen coming in—he let me put the cannula in his nose. Shortly after this, our friend, Reverend Tina, arrived to provide counsel and comfort. Tina, Bernie's son, Bernie's friend Hans, and I formed a circle around Bernie as he sat on the lower right corner of his bed. Then Tina began praying and sending him healing energy. I told him he was free to leave—everyone and everything would be fine, and God was anticipating his arrival, along with his family and friends. He could simply let go.

I crawled in front of his lap, bent over, made eye contact one last time, smiled, and said goodbye. He nodded his head ever so slightly, squeezed my hand three times, telling me I LOVE YOU, and then took his final breath. His soul was liberated from his body—he was free.

Bernie's presence and large spirit immediately filled the room with the most exquisite, divine, pristine energy I had ever felt, as if all the angels in the universe were present, singing his praises. Tears of ecstasy and happiness for him overcame me.

We were silent for a few minutes—none of us wanted to move. We all held hands in honor of this exceptional moment we shared. I am bonded forever with Tina, Hans, and Bernie's son.

It was the most magnificent, sacred experience of my life.

Part 1

Me and My Beloved Bernie

This is the story of my life with my Beloved Bernie, my experience of his death, and creating a life without him. I recount the wonders and the struggles of our amazing ten years together, the journey of our final eight months, and how I championed my future over the next five years. I invite you into the extraordinary chapters of my life as I share many gems along the way about what I did and how I took care of myself before, during, and after Bernie's passing.

I first met Bernie in October 2003, at a personal development course called the *Landmark Forum®*. My life was at a point where I wanted to expand the effectiveness of my communications and improve the quality of my relationships. After the weekend course, we both took part in a 10-week seminar series, along with other Forum participants. He was married, so I paid little attention to him during the meetings.

Bernie and I both happened to attend a Christmas party hosted by one of the people in the seminar. Sitting at the kitchen island, we talked for hours, like no one else was in the room. I shared with him about my transformational healing practice, *Center for Extraordinary Outcomes*, which I opened in 1996. I explained the *Resonance Repatterning®* process I offered and taught, along with other unique healing methods I added over the years. I also expressed my strong desire to relax on beaches around the world. I love being at the beach—wide open spaces, fresh air, walking along the shore, and collecting seashells where the waves meet the sand.

Bernie told me about his plan to play a lot of golf and travel extensively, which was why he had two part-time jobs. One, working at a golf course so he could play for free, and another as an airline ground agent, so he could fly standby, inexpensively. He was doing what he loved and was happy. Our conversation was interesting, impactful, and memorable. We didn't speak again for several years.

In the spring of 2007, I started receiving emails from sunpower11. I knew it wasn't wise to open an unfamiliar email address. My intuition told me to open it anyway and I'm glad I did—the messages were uplifting and empowering. These inspirational emails came every few days—then one day, the email began with, "*Just for You!*"

Being bold, I thanked whomever it was for the uplifting messages that truly made a difference in my life, and inquired, "*Do I know you? Should I know you?*"

"*Yes, it's Bernie, from the Landmark Forum courses we participated in four years ago, remember me? I want to learn more about the work you do, and I know some people who might be interested. When can we get together?*"

I looked at my schedule and saw that I was available that day for lunch, so I asked, "*Is today too soon?*"

"*Nope, today would be perfect.*"

Bernie brought over Chinese food and we talked for three hours non-stop. Our conversation focused on my healing work. I explained how I help people identify and release the emotional and mental patterns holding them back from having what they want in life. Then support them in aligning with new patterns to accomplish their goals. I always loved talking about my work because my clients experienced highly inspirational results.

The discussion also included our spiritual history. I shared about being raised in the Catholic Church, then connecting in my mid-twenties with Unity Chicago Church. After I moved to Arizona, I attended the Unity of Phoenix Spiritual Center. In addition, I revealed my deep and heartfelt connection with God and the gift of being able to hear His voice and capture

God's profound messages in my journal. This made my contemplative prayer time very special.

Bernie disclosed that he also had been raised in the Catholic Church, then participated in Reverend Moon's Unification Church in his mid-twenties for 15 years and for the last several years, has been attending the Unity of Phoenix Spiritual Center. It meant a lot to us that we were aligned spiritually, and we wondered why we had never crossed paths with each other at church.

Bernie shared that he had two arranged marriages during his time with The Unification Church and had gotten divorced in 2004 from his wife of fifteen years. He also told me his rebound relationship had been over for a year. This was a good thing since I had two important rules about dating— men are married until their divorce is final and no dating anyone on the rebound. Sharing experiences can be fun and the sex might be great, but the heartache is often greater and, frankly, not worth it.

As he was leaving, Bernie asked if I wanted to meet at my house again on Saturday night. I did, so we did.

The doorbell rang. I opened the door with great anticipation. There stood Bernie with strawberry shortcake and a bottle of wine. Without even saying hello, he announced, *"I only want to be your friend."*

I was taken aback. Not knowing exactly how to respond, I said, *"I don't know what the future brings, but I do know that I like to get to know someone first before starting any kind of romantic relationship."*

"Great, I'll let you know if I change my mind."

Later that evening, Bernie shared he didn't want me to think he was coming over just to get laid, which he figured most men would try to do. My impression, at this point, was that he had strong ethics about relationships and was highly respectful—which proved to be true.

We spent the next month having so much fun, just hanging out as friends. He taught me to play golf, which I had never done—except for the miniature version. I loved it! We were both hikers and took several invigorating walks on local mountain paths. We also made day trips in Arizona, always listening to enjoyable music on the way. I specifically remember the second time we went to the Apache Trail for a picnic—Bernie brought strawberries and whipped cream for dessert. I remarked, *"This is pretty sensual for a platonic picnic."* He just smiled.

Whenever we met up, we'd talk about our upbringing, careers, hobbies, likes, dislikes, friendships, and past romantic relationships. We learned so much about each other—the good, the bad, and the ugly. Bernie could count on one hand the women he'd been with, and my relationship history was full of men. When he asked me to reveal details of my past relationships, I told him that the only way I would share these experiences was if he would celebrate what I learned and who I'd become because of them. He agreed and got an earful—including lots of laughter and a few tears.

About five weeks after we first had dinner at my house, we drove out to Bartlett Lake. We were lying on a beach towel after swimming, and he leaned over and kissed me. I said, *"Oh, you changed your mind, did you?"*

"Yep." The kiss was delicious—our loving relationship had begun. He became my Beloved Bernie.

As our connection deepened, we slowly shared our hearts' desires and what each of us wanted for our future. We discovered we had different, yet compatible dreams—similar enough to move forward together. I was hoping for at least forty years, I got ten—the best ten years of my life.

After I met Bernie, I started putting a priority on having fun, traveling, and spending time with family. I began scheduling work around plans with him, rather than fitting our time together around my work. It was a complete shift in my mindset from being driven by my career and making money to sharing a glorious life with him—which is exactly what happened.

Each New Year's Day, Bernie and I would create and declare our intentions for the coming year. Getting clear about, writing down, and communicating our plans for the future was a powerful way to manifest what we wanted to accomplish.

We always included the standards we strived to live by that made everything else in our lives possible. Bernie's was fulfilling his life's purpose to be his greatest and highest self—loving, kind, joyful, and adventurous. Mine were living a heart-centered life, thriving as a human being rather than a human doing, and taking care of myself along the way. All while fulfilling my purpose to inspire and empower myself and others to live extraordinary lives, overflowing with love, adventure, passion, and joy.

We discussed what we each needed and how we could encourage one another. It was such a lovely coming together—a way we could work to be the best versions of ourselves while contributing to and supporting each other's greatness.

We talked about all the lovely places we wanted to visit and then laid out a travel schedule for the year. We had a lot of flexibility since I worked for myself and Bernie worked for the airlines.

Taking care of my well-being was important to me. I regularly had physical therapy, acupuncture, and massage for a shoulder injury I sustained in 1990. To expand my knowledge and wisdom, I attended workshops and conferences, along with personal reading for pure entertainment. Meditation, hiking, riding my bike, and dancing every chance I got, centered me in my heart. When I started writing in 2011, I set aside time for book writing retreats to ensure my inspiration never stopped flowing. During 2014, I began singing weekly in the Higher Vibrations choir that fed my soul.

Bernie found immense pleasure in getting a great deal. He checked out yard sales, shopped thrift stores, and scoured online sites whenever he could. He also loved online poker, playing golf, and researching aspects of spirituality that interested him.

Living separately during our first six years together genuinely supported both of us. We were always brimming with anticipation and excitement for the weekend because we weren't in each other's hair during the week. We integrated our lives, including visiting my mom, spending time with his sons, and attending Unity Church. Much of our social life included his best friend Robert, my best friend Linda, and several other people in our individual lives—connecting, laughing, and being joyful, whether we were at the movies, out to dinner, or just hanging out.

Friday evenings were special to us—it's when the fun began! I remember running to my front door when Bernie rang the bell—it was thrilling to see him again after being apart all week. Sometimes he would bring the groceries for dinner and we'd create appetizing meals at home. Other times we would go out to a restaurant for delicious meals without having to do the work. Twice a month, after we ate, we attended spiritual channeling sessions.

On the first Friday of the month, we were regulars at Intuitive Directions' Equinoxx sessions, channeled by Joan Scibienski. Bernie and I had the privilege of sitting at the front of the room with Joan. His thirst for knowledge and answers surpassed anyone I knew, which was often satisfied by Equinoxx. On the way home from these gatherings, he and I would talk about all the knowledge that was shared and what we learned. Sometimes we would even create more questions for the next month's gathering. We loved sharing these moments.

On the last Friday of each month, we were also regulars at Torina, channeled through Brenda Fulkerson. We especially valued these sessions as they provided more opportunities to discuss and get clarity about the answers to our questions. Knowing Torina would send us healing energy for three days, I intentionally connected with this energy before I went to sleep, when I woke up, and often throughout the day.

We did our best to integrate into our daily lives everything we received through these channeling sessions, both personally and as a couple. It was delightful to be with a man who genuinely enjoyed being with other people and was interested in exploring spiritual perspectives that were not traditional.

We traveled easily together and shared a multitude of adventures, whether it was in Arizona, out of state, or out of the country. Our Arizona day trips included visiting all the popular tourist spots and towns—the Grand Canyon, Tonto National Forest, Apache Trail, Sedona, Prescott, and Jerome were some of our favorites. Going to The London Bridge in Lake Havasu and picnicking at local area lakes were especially fun.

Having lived in the metropolitan Midwest until I was 36, I loved the desert from the start. The wide-open spaces and mountains, with blooming cacti, wildflowers galore, and impressive views, provided a serenity all its own. One of our trips to Sedona stands out in my memory.

I was the early bird and always had plenty of time to prepare our lunch. For this trip, I made a big salad with lots of veggies and cold rotisserie chicken, which I knew Bernie would love. When he got up, he loaded the cooler and our folding chairs in the trunk, and off we went. We both loved to drive. I would drive first while Bernie's coffee kicked in. Half way there, we stopped to get more coffee and switch drivers. We took our time, admiring the beautiful scenery, for which the area is famous.

As usual, Bernie found a secluded spot to stop for our picnic, right along the shore of Oak Creek. It was incredibly quiet and peaceful. We ate my tasty salad, and then sat holding hands, mesmerized by the beauty of the moment. I surprised him by pulling out one of his favorite spiritual books and began reading aloud. He always loved this, and I could tell from his smile that he was happy. Within twenty minutes he was asleep, so I stopped reading. The fresh air and gentle wind quickly put me to sleep as well. We woke up about an hour later and drove to our favorite nearby hiking spot and went for a short walk.

What made this trip so memorable was the sensational double rainbow we saw on the way home—it was breathtaking. We parked on the side of the road for a few minutes to soak it up.

Bernie's cabin in the former mining town of Breezy Pines, Arizona, was one of our top five places to go because it was considerably cooler in the summer and just over an hour from home. We often took 3-day weekends there.

The breeze would whisper through the tall pines, hence the name Breezy Pines. Sometimes we'd pack a lunch and take long hikes, exploring the surrounding area. Other times, we'd get on his 4-wheeler ATV and go on a longer adventure. Once in a while we visited Old Man Carl, who made the best Bloody Mary in town which we drank in the middle of the afternoon no less. Many evenings we would eat lots of nummy food then drink red wine as we enjoyed gazing at the fire in the fireplace.

Occasionally, we invited friends to come with us for the weekend, which was also a ton of fun. A few times, we enthusiastically mingled with the other summer residents at the local Labor Day party.

Adventures abounded because Bernie worked for an airline and we could fly standby. It gave us the opportunity for extensive travel to other parts of the world. Stateside, we visited Florida, California, and Nevada, among others. We also went to Wisconsin and Wyoming to visit my brother and sisters. We took six trips to Hawaii visiting Maui, Kona, and Kauai—we liked Kauai the best. Mexico was a frequent destination—we alternated between Cancun, Los Cabos, Puerto Vallarta, and Puerto Penasco. We also shared many adventures in Germany, Austria, St. Lucia, and Belize, our second favorite location.

Whenever we went to a beach, we'd spend time just looking out over the water toward the horizon. On some beaches, the waves peacefully rolled in and gently kissed the shore, on others they roared and crashed onto the sand, reverberating with power. I preferred the calm and Bernie preferred the intensity. We did both, holding hands and talking about the vastness of Mother Nature and the gratitude we felt to have the time, money, energy, and health to visit so many fabulous beaches. We always had a blast!

Bernie made all the travel plans. He'd find deals that I never imagined even existed. Yes, we sat in several timeshare presentations and took advantage of one trial offer that I eventually used. Flying standby was an experience in itself—there was always a chance we wouldn't be able to fly together or even go at all. We'd check the flights the night before, then sometimes by the morning our seats were gone—bummer! We didn't wish anyone harm, although we often hoped people were having such a great time that they'd choose to stay longer in the city we were trying to leave.

Bernie was much more laid back than I was. I always wanted a Plan B. What if there was only one seat? Would we fly separately or wait for another flight? What if there were no seats? Would we be adventurous and pick a place we could get seats to, or wait for the next flight to our destination? Only twice did we choose to go on separate flights and, regrettably, we never opted for a different location.

Through all our ups and downs traveling, Bernie and I never let the circumstances interfere with our happiness. We enjoyed being together no matter what we were doing. One of our more challenging excursions was our second trip to Kauai.

This trip included Bernie's younger brother, his wife, and their two adult children. We all got along famously and had an incredible vacation. When it was time to leave, there were six of us trying to get back to Phoenix traveling standby—what a mess. As an airline employee, Bernie had a decent chance of getting us all to the top of the list for the nightly red-eye. He spent considerable time every day looking for options—direct flights, flying to another island first, any route he could find, then hoping for the best. On the nights we had good odds to make it home, we would pack up, drive to the airport, leave the car where it could be picked up by us or the rental company, and then wait, hoping we could get on the flight. As we were never sure we were leaving, Bernie had to arrange with the hotel to hold our rooms and with the car rental agency to extend our reservation. When we finally left, I had to fly to Kona first, while everyone else flew direct—real bummer.

Although I was frustrated, I was very glad to be going home. It had taken seven days after our original departure date for everyone to return to Phoenix.

In January 2015, just one year after the family travel fiasco, Bernie and I headed off for a third trip to Kauai—our favorite place in the world, with its lush gardens, hundreds of waterfalls, and phenomenal beaches. Our plan was to camp at several locations around the island.

Bernie's status with the airline meant we could each check two 50-pound suitcases, and so we did. Two of the four suitcases contained all we could possibly need to set up our campsite, be comfortable, and prepare food. We packed a tent, an inflatable mattress, two back-jack chairs, flashlight, candles, matches, plastic ware and paper plates, corkscrew, can opener, sharp knives, instant coffee, and sugar. We planned to buy anything else we needed after we got there.

Our personal items filled the other two suitcases: books, playing cards, towels and wash cloths, swimsuits, tennis shoes, sandals, first-aid kit, snorkeling gear, water shoes, suntan lotion, bug spray, sunhats, fanny packs, and more. Since we were going to Hawaii's rainiest island, we also took our rain gear. The weather was unpredictable, so I chose warm clothes for the evening and summer things for daytime. Needless to say, I brought way too much.

Standby was always risky—a risk well worth taking! Yay, we got on the flight and arrived at the Lihue airport in Kauai seven hours later.

We grabbed some travel maps at the airport, picked up our rental car, and were off to Costco to buy a week's worth of groceries and supplies. Since we didn't have a camping stove, we couldn't do any cooking, so we bought a rotisserie chicken, prepared salads, trail mix, almonds, cans of tuna, lots of local fruit, and of course, red wine. A styrofoam cooler and plenty of ice were added to keep the food fresh.

The first week we camped on the southwest side of the island, then moved to the northwest side for the second week. They have a rule in Kauai that no one can stay at any beach campsite for more than three nights. We became experts at quickly packing up, moving, and resetting our campsite in another location.

First, we headed to Polihale, the longest beach in all the Hawaiian Islands. We drove up and found a campsite right on the beach—perfect place for three nights. On arrival, we noticed one group of campers next to us were naked! So, after we put up our tent, naked we got!

This camping area was the most serene of all. It was so far away from everything, few people came to check it out. We spent our days exploring the nearby hiking trails, walking on the beach, reading, and relaxing. One afternoon, we drove a short way to Barking Sounds Beach. Its name comes from the sound the sand sometimes makes when it slides down the sixty-foot high dunes along the beach—we loved it.

Wednesday morning, we packed up and headed to a campground in Kekaha Kai State Park for two nights. It's known for sandy beaches and hiking trails—we took full advantage of both, loving every minute! Did I mention the sunsets were astonishing?

On Thursday, we drove over to spend the day in Waimea. We explored the beaches, rather than going inland to see the city's sites. Did I tell you we loved beaches?

Friday, we loaded the car and went off to Hanapepe to hang out for three days at Salt Pond Beach Park, known for *its gentle waves and clear water. Despite Kauai being the rainy island, surprisingly, it seldom rains there, even when it's pouring everywhere else. Generations of indigenous families have produced Hawaiian natural sea salt from the ponds near the beach—hence the name.*

After we set up camp, we walked down to Crescent Beach and took advantage of the awesome snorkeling it provided—the first opportunity we had on our trip. We also watched the salt tide pools, where water shoots fifteen feet straight up in the air.

Friday night, we went to the Hanapepe Market and Art Night, the best time to wander through town—all the art galleries were open, and the shops and restaurants were bustling. Outside each restaurant was a food truck where we could sample their delicious cooking. We were glad to see Connie and Arnie, who we met the last time we were in Kauai—they had a booth selling jewelry for a friend. We spent some time hanging out with the locals, who were having a jam session—great entertainment and fun. Afterward, we perused the Talk Story Bookstore—the westernmost bookstore in the United States. This is where I got the idea to come back and have a book signing after I published my first book.

On Sunday morning, we drove to the airport to exchange our rental car, then stopped to visit Bernie's friend Georgio and his family. His entire backyard was a massive aquaponic garden. He took us through it and explained everything and how it worked—we were awestruck. That evening, we visited the Buddhist temple with Georgio and his family. Listening to so many people chanting Buddhist prayers was a unique and uplifting experience for us. We ended up staying at Georgio's house on a comfortable bed in their renovated garage. It was nice and relaxing—my back was extremely happy!

In the morning, we stopped once again at Costco and bought another week's worth of food for the next leg of our trip up the Royal Coconut Coast.

The drive to our first destination, Anahola Beach Park, was breathtaking. It's known for its beautiful white sand, as well as good swimming and snorkeling, both of which we did. As with my previous snorkeling experiences, seeing the living world under the water was beautiful and captivating. We spent Monday and Tuesday evening camping right on the beach. I had to pinch myself most days to make sure I wasn't dreaming.

Wednesday morning, we were off to Kilauea, which is inland several miles off the northern coastline. Bernie arranged for us to camp for two nights on his friend Gene's property— we arrived just in time for lunch. Gene had a large community kitchen and dining room which served his Airbnb guests and the college students who worked in his garden in exchange for room and board. Everyone was so friendly and contributed to the huge spread of food—it was delightful.

After lunch, Bernie and I spent precious time together enjoying the nearby beach. We returned several hours later to another wonderful community meal, then retreated to our tent by the stream beyond the garden. It was so peaceful, and I loved hearing the flowing water as we drifted off to sleep.

During our days there, we drove to two local beaches to read, relax, and frolic in the ocean. I was in heaven! In the evenings, everyone got together for dinner, games, interesting conversation, and wine. When they asked about the healing work I do, I brought out my Repatterning Process Guide, then explained how it worked and the benefits. They were all enthralled. I gave Gene a session on Thursday—he was overjoyed about the new possibilities he could expect in his life.

On Friday, we left Gene's and moved farther west to Anini Beach Park. The longest reef in Hawaii runs the length of the beach, making it one of the safest and most protected beaches along the North Shore. After we settled at the campground, we drove a few miles to my friend Carol's home in Ha'ena. We had a delightful visit and a delicious lunch—I was glad we took the time to see her. When we came back to our campsite, we went snorkeling—the underwater scenery was breathtaking! We spent that evening with the other campers around a huge bonfire, appreciating the stimulating conversation, wine, cheese, and outstanding music!

On Saturday, we drove to Napali Coast State Wilderness Park and took the day-hike from Ke'e Beach to Hanakāpī'ai Beach. Walking along the cliff above the beach was deeply moving, exceptionally beautiful, and left me in awe of Mother Nature. We returned to our campsite and had our usual dinner. While I was falling asleep, I began reminiscing about our time in Kauai. As I felt the soft breeze and the sound of the waves lapping on the shore, I really didn't want to go home.

We got up Sunday morning, packed up and headed down the coast to Lihue. Since Georgio lived near the airport, we spent the last day at his place. His front yard was the scene of reorganizing and packing our suitcases to make sure none of them were overweight. To make room for the things we bought, we donated camping equipment we didn't want to take home. We returned the rental car and luckily grabbed the last two standby seats on the red-eye. God was watching over us! We had a safe journey and arrived in Phoenix at 6:00 in the morning on Monday. After we got home, I tried to stay awake, but by 1:00 I could no longer keep my eyes open—and while Bernie always slept like a baby—I am rarely able to fall *asleep on planes. I took a long nap, unpacked, and started to reintegrate into my day-to-day life. This was a trip of a lifetime! We planned to return—we never had the chance.*

Before I met Bernie, I had only traveled internationally once, when I taught a Resonance Repatterning course in Wales. It was always interesting and exciting to take vacations to Europe with Bernie and experience other cultures. The second time we went to Germany was in the summer.

I loved being in an environment that was so different from Phoenix. It was green with rolling hills and many small towns.

We arrived on a Friday. Bernie and I joined his youngest brother and his wife to spend the weekend with family friends in Zell am See in Salzburg, Austria. It was gorgeous—the streets were lined with quaint houses that had window boxes all around filled with flowers in full bloom. The food was delicious, and the beer was flowing! I had to rely on Bernie to translate what everyone was saying. Sometimes he was so engaged in the conversation, he forgot to translate for me—it was frustrating. I kept poking him and asking, "What are you taking about?"

Saturday, we drove to the base of Schmittenhöhe mountain on the eastern edge of the Kitzbühel Alps. The local residents and visitors could enjoy skiing in the winter and hiking in the summer—the best of both worlds. We rode the cable car up to the top, took a long hike, and stopped at the cafe to have lunch. The view was spectacular!

The next day we visited Sigmund-Thun Klamm in the Austrian Alps, an impressive mountain gorge, with plenty of waterfalls and dramatic views that we walked through on a wooden pathway. The water was roaring below us, fast and furious.

My favorite adventure was on Monday. We took a boat cruise around Lake Zell, taking in the views of the mountain and the lake side promenade. It was delightful seeing so many people enjoying themselves. After the cruise, we walked through some of the charming shops and ate at a local restaurant—it was wonderful.

What a fabulous trip!

A major reason Bernie and I lived separately for six years and rarely spent time at Bernie's place was because of all the clutter on the inside and outside of his home. I remember mentioning to him that I could never live in his environment. To know Bernie was to know that he had a generous and charitable heart. Where Bernie saw valuable treasures—that could be useful to others or sold for a profit—I saw worthless junk. The backyard looked like a trash heap and there were areas in the house that were almost impassable. He had hundreds of ideas for projects to make money, which he never quite started or finished. Eliminating his accumulation of frivolous stuff was not even on his list of things to think about, much less to release. It was a bone of contention between us.

Bernie's house was a 1700 sq ft, three-bedroom, two-bath, ranch style on a corner lot. He had converted the garage into a 600 sq ft apartment for his sons. It had a separate entrance and foyer, a bedroom, a living room, a small space for a kitchen, a bathroom, and the family laundry room, all with no heat or air conditioning. There was a sliding door between the apartment and the main house. The backyard was huge with a diving pool and a covered patio ran along the entire back of the house.

With a keen eye, Bernie was always finding smokin' deals at yard and estate sales, in addition to relentlessly searching on Amazon, eBay, and Craig's List. He also often shopped at Goodwill for items he thought might be useful or could be repaired and sold. His intention was to make huge profits by reselling the things he bought, yet he rarely sold anything. The clutter just kept growing—I knew the source of this went deeper than what was on the surface. I asked him why he had so much stuff everywhere and why he wasn't clearing it out. He said he wanted to keep things in case someone, someday, needed something, which rarely happened. I acknowledged his good intentions, reminded him it was not his job to supply everyone with what they needed, and that his main responsibility was to take care of himself first. Eventually, I found out that he surrounded himself with stuff to replace the love he thought was missing in his life.

In early 2013, Bernie and I talked about having a commitment ceremony and he said, *"I'll let you know when I'm ready."* We also discussed getting our own home. He promised me that he would clear out and sell his house as soon as possible. I acted immediately, sold my condo, gave my furniture to a refugee family, and packed up the rest of my household belongings, which I stored on his back patio.

When my condo sold, Bernie's oldest adult son was staying at his house, so I rented a friend's spare room until he moved out and I could move in. Before I moved in, Bernie had taken no action on his promise to start clearing the space or selling the house. I was hoping my being there would inspire him to do what was needed to sell his place.

Moving Day, July 4—fireworks, the perfect celebration. I was finally living with my beloved. Unfortunately, Bernie snored loudly, so it was important for both of us to have our own space. We enjoyed sparate bedrooms which really worked for us. Within two days, Bernie reached across the kitchen table unexpectedly, held my hands, looked into my eyes, and said, *"I love you, Victoria. I am ready to have a commitment ceremony."*

It took my breath away. With tears of joy welling up, and my love pouring into his eyes, I asked, *"When?"*—I thought for sure he'd say sometime next month. He said, *"Tomorrow."*

"TOMORROW!?"

"Yes, tomorrow."

"Yikes stripes, REALLY? How exciting—let's go for it!"

As soon as I said yes, Bernie called his friend Christopher and asked if he would officiate our commitment ceremony, he gladly agreed.

Christopher called his friend, Kirsta, who was renting a house that had a cute backyard. He asked her if she wanted to take part in making this a special day for us. She said yes, then called her next door neighbor who agreed to be our wedding photographer. Without me even knowing it or having to lift a finger, location and photos—check.

In the meantime, I was frantically making a mental list of all the things that needed to be done before the wedding could even begin. What am I wearing? Do I have the right shoes? What about flowers, music, food, rings, and most importantly our vows? So much to do!!! We didn't have time to invite anyone, so no worries about invitations and RSVPs.

Since Bernie's previous marriages had been arranged, it was extra special that he was making his own choice to spend his life with me, out of all the women he had ever met. Bride and groom—check.

Our next step was to download a copy of Neale Donald Walsch's wedding vows. It only took us a couple of hours to create the ceremony we desired and the vows that sincerely expressed our commitment to each other. What we designed was as unconventional as we were. Vows—check.

Saturday morning, July 7, 2013, the BIG DAY! What to wear? I thought I knew since I had bought a dress several years earlier, thinking it would be perfect to get married in someday. It was bright peach, cocktail length, sleeveless, low cut, and fitted to show every curve. We went to my closet, and I pulled out the dress. Bernie proclaimed, *"Fashion show!"* Once I had it on, unfortunately he wasn't thrilled.

I asked my beloved what he was thinking of wearing. He said, *"My favorite Hawaiian shirt, representing all the fun we've shared whenever we visited Hawaii."*

"Great idea!"

Knowing what he was wearing we continued looking through my closet. The perfect Hawaiian sundress took my breath away. I put it on—it was THE ONE. Then, I found the perfect shoes and straw hat. Dress, shoes, hat—check.

Given that we only had one day to prepare, we used two gold rings we found among our personal jewelry. Rings—check.

We planned to take everyone out for dinner afterward. Food—check.

Bernie and I put our wedding clothes in a garment bag, made sure we had the rings, and away we went. We stopped at the store to get champagne and three roses for our ceremony, two pink and one white. Champagne and flowers—check.

When we walked into Kirsta's home, the magic began—it was ALL perfect. They had decorated the living room with twinkle lights. On the dining table, there was a charming wedding card, a loving message created with scrabble letters, two glasses of red wine ready for us, and a huge bowl of Christopher's homemade Asian chicken salad for after the ceremony. It was so special.

Christopher and Kirsta were musicians and, unbeknownst to us, they stayed up until midnight the night before, writing a song just for our special day. Christopher picked up his guitar, and they both sang their heartfelt song as we drank the refreshing and delicious wine. Music—check.

After the surprise serenade, we tied our wedding rings to the pink roses and placed them, along with the white rose, on the table. We gave Christopher our vows so he could read them over before we started. Then the photographer arrived—great surprise.

We changed into our wedding outfits and picked up the roses on our way outside to stand beneath the large tree in the backyard. I was honored they had both lovingly gone to such lengths to make our special day spectacular. Particularly Kirsta, who had never met us. I was as happy as a fish in water! So much love filled my heart I thought it would burst.

Our commitment ceremony began.

Christopher:

"Bernhard and Victoria have come here to make their love for each other known, to give a voice to their truth; to live and grow together, and to declare their choice out loud. It is their desire that we come to feel a very real and intimate part of their decision, and this makes it even more powerful.

They have also come here today in the further hope that their ritual of bonding will help bring us all closer together. Let this ceremony be a reminder, a rededication of your own loving bonds with family and friends.

This is the Ceremony of Roses, in which Bernhard and Victoria share their understandings, and commemorate that sharing.

Now, Bernhard and Victoria, you have told me it is your firm understanding that you are not entering into this commitment for reasons of security; that the only real security is not in owning or possessing, nor in being owned or possessed; not in demanding or expecting; and not even in hoping that what you think you need in life will be supplied by the other; but rather, in knowing that everything you need in life—all the love, all the wisdom, all the knowledge, all the understanding, all the nurturing, all the compassion, and all the strength— resides within you and that you are not committing to the other in hopes of getting these things, but in hopes of giving these gifts, that the other might have them in even greater abundance. Is that your firm understanding today?"

Bernie & I Responded:

   "It is."

Christopher:

   "And Bernhard and Victoria, you have told me it is your firm understanding that you are not entering into this commitment as a means of in any way limiting, controlling, hindering, or restricting each other from any true expression and honest celebration of that which is the highest and best you—including your love of God, your love of life, your love of people, your love of creativity; your love of work, golf, dancing, and any aspect of being which genuinely represents you and brings you joy. Is that your firm understanding today?"

Bernie & I Responded:

   "It is."

Christopher:

"Finally, Victoria and Bernhard, you have said to me that you do not see commitment as producing obligations, but rather as providing opportunities, opportunities for growth and full self-expression; for lifting your lives to their highest potential; for healing every false thought or small idea you ever had about yourself; and for ultimate reunion with God through the communion of your two souls. This is truly a Holy Communion—a journey through life with the one you love as an equal partner. Sharing equally both the authority and the responsibilities inherent in any partnership; bearing equally what burdens there may be; and basking equally in the glories.

Is that the vision you wish to enter into now?"

Bernie & I Responded:

"It is."

Christopher handed us each the pink rose with our own ring on it.

Christopher:

"I now give you these pink roses, symbolizing your individual understandings of these opportunities; that you both know and agree how life will be within the structure of your commitment, as you both intend it.

Give these roses now to each other as a symbol of your sharing of these agreements and understandings with love and tenderness.

Now, please, hold the white rose together. It is a symbol of your larger understanding of your spiritual nature and your spiritual truth. It stands for the purity of your Real and Highest Self, and of the purity of God's love, which shines upon you now and always.

What symbols do you bring as a reminder of the commitment given and received today?"

We handed the white rose back to Christopher, and we each removed the ring from the stem of the pink rose we were holding.

Christopher:

"A circle is the symbol of the Sun, and the Earth, and the Universe. It is a symbol of holiness, and of perfection and peace. It is also the symbol of the eternity of spiritual truth, love, and life—that which has no beginning and no end. And in this moment, Victoria and Bernhard choose for it to also be a symbol of unity, but not of possession; of joining, but not of restricting; of encirclement, but not of entrapment. For love cannot be possessed, nor can it be restricted. And the soul can never be entrapped.

Please exchange your rings and repeat after me."

Bernie & I Repeated:

"I now take the ring you give to me, and give it a place upon my hand, that all may see it and know of our love for each other."

Christopher:

"We recognize with full awareness that only a couple can administer the commitment of partnership to each other, and only a couple can sanctify it. Neither the church, nor any power vested in me, can grant me the authority to declare what only two hearts can declare, and what only two souls can make real. And so now, inasmuch as you, Victoria, and you, Bernhard, have announced the truths that are already written in your hearts, and have witnessed the same in the presence of your

friends, and the One Living Spirit—we observe joyfully that you have declared yourselves to be Partners in Love and Life.

Let us now join in prayer.

Spirit of Love and Life: out of this whole world, two souls have found each other. Their destinies shall now be woven into one design. Bernhard and Victoria, may your home be a place of happiness for all who enter it; a place where the old and the young are renewed in each other's company; a place for growing and a place for sharing; a place for music and a place for laughter; a place for prayer and a place for love. May those who are nearest to you be constantly enriched by the beauty and the bounty of your love for one another. May your work be a joy that serves the world, and may your days be good and long upon the Earth. Amen and amen."

Christopher was so excited that he pronounced us Partners in Love and Life before we actually exchanged our vows. I kindly reminded him that we weren't done yet, and that it was deeply meaningful to be able to express what I wanted to say to Bernie and to hear what he wanted to say to me. We resumed the ceremony in the waning light of the afternoon.

Christopher:

"Victoria, please repeat after me."

I Repeated:

"I, Victoria, ask you Bernhard, to be my partner, my lover, and my friend. I announce and declare my intention to give you my deepest friendship and love, not only when your moments are high, but when they are low; not only when you remember clearly Who You Are, but when you forget; not only when you are acting with love, but when you are not. I further announce, before God and those here present, that I will seek always to see the Light of Divinity within you and seek always to share the Light of Divinity within me, even and especially, in whatever moments of darkness may come. It is my intention to be with you all the days of your life in a Holy Partnership of the Soul—that we may do together God's work, sharing all that is good within us with all those whose lives we touch."

Christopher:

"Bernhard, do you choose to grant Victoria's request that you be her partner in life?"

Bernie Responded:

"I do."

Christopher:

"Bernhard, please repeat after me."

Bernie Repeated:

"I, Bernhard, ask you Victoria, to be my partner, my lover, and my friend. I announce and declare my intention to

give you my deepest friendship and love, not only when your moments are high, but when they are low; not only when you remember clearly Who You Are, but when you forget; not only when you are acting with love, but when you are not. I further announce, before God and those here present, that I will seek always to see the Light of Divinity within you and seek always to share the Light of Divinity within me, even and especially, in whatever moments of darkness may come. It is my intention to be with you all the days of your life in a Holy Partnership of the Soul—that we may do together God's work, sharing all that is good within us with all those whose lives we touch."

Christopher:

"Victoria, do you choose to grant Bernhard's request that you be his partner in life?"

I Responded:

"I do."

Our vows were complete—we were Partners in Love & Life by declaration.

After the ceremony, the photographer took a few pictures of us outside. We spent the rest of the afternoon and early evening enjoying the delicious food, flowing champagne, excellent music, and deep conversations. Christopher gave an inspiring toast, including some wise words for the success of our relationship.

Our time living together was mostly wonderful. The most important thing that made it work so well was that we granted each other freedom.

I love to dance and regularly took dance lessons at The Fatcat Ballroom. Bernie loved to play poker. He often played free money poker online and—like all poker players—he won some and lost some.

I loved to go to Tom Bird's, *Write Your Best-Seller in a Weekend* retreats in Sedona. Starting in 2011, I attended seven times and wrote seven books. Bernie loved to ski. He sometimes went to northern Arizona or Utah for ski weekends and he always had a blast!

I loved taking part most Mondays in the Higher Vibrations choir, where people gather to sing from their heart and connect with each other. Bernie loved to play golf and teed off every chance he got.

I'm a morning person—early to bed, early to rise. Bernie was a night owl—in bed at 2:00 in the morning, up at 10:00. I was already at my office seeing clients when he was waking up, so it worked out perfectly—we each had the alone time we needed.

There was no question about our love and commitment—there was total trust. Some people think commitment ties you down—we felt it granted freedom, and for us it did.

Bernie showed his love for me by being ready to lend me a helping hand whenever he could. Anytime I promoted my transformational healing business at an event, he was there to support me. I would gather and pack the supplies I needed—my vendor table, manuals, posters, flyers, pens, sales equipment, etc. Bernie would get it all into the car then carry everything into the location, unpack, and help me setup the display table. He would sit right beside me—anything I needed, he was ready and willing to do. While I was giving mini sessions at the end of the table, he engaged genuinely with the interested people who came by my booth. I was proud to have him by my side.

I showed my love for Bernie more through the small things, which seemed to have a powerful emotional effect on him. He appreciated my smile; my sincere friendship; my words of encouragement; my happy, upbeat, optimistic way of being; and my kind, nurturing nature. He enjoyed getting a great deal and loved it when I went with him to shop at Goodwill and browse yard sales. Even though he was uncomfortable when I held him accountable for his words and actions, I know deep down he admired me for it. For the most part, I was genuinely supportive, understanding, and compassionate. The primary exception was when it came to his overwhelming clutter.

Bernie mostly went with the flow in life, yet he had a stubborn streak, especially when it came to caring for himself. I persisted and did my best to support him in releasing clutter in the apartment and our backyard, as well as taking better care of his home and health.

Neither of us liked confrontation, so we did our best to work things out before they became troublesome. We made sure to discuss any concern or dissatisfaction as it arose. We would sincerely apologize as needed, which made living together more harmonious—even with all the clutter.

My style was to use Alison Armstrong's *Needs Conversation* that I learned in her **Understanding Men**® workshop. This is how it worked: I'd get clear about what I wanted to talk about. Then, I would approach Bernie when he wasn't busy, let him know I had something important to share, and ask when he would be available. I began our conversations by acknowledging and appreciating him for those special things he had done for me. I then shared what was on my mind, what I needed, when I would like to have it done, and asked him if he was willing to accept my request. He usually said yes and sometimes requested more time to complete it. I'd thank him and ask whether he needed anything from me to make completing my request easier.

Bernie had a different style when he had an important matter to discuss. He would simply tell me what was on his mind during the course of daily activities. If he wanted to talk when I was busy, I would ask him to wait until I was free to give him my full attention, and we could address his concern thoroughly.

Both ways of handling these conversations worked well for us. Don't get me wrong, it wasn't perfect, we had our moments. Mostly our moments were about his stuff filling up the house and my lack of availability due to how much time I spent working on my business and my creative writing projects. I am so grateful for the ten years we shared. Most couples don't even get close to the love we experienced together. I am so blessed.

After our wedding, Bernie had told me to shop for a ring, since we didn't have time before the ceremony. In early 2015, I was ready and took him at his word. A local jewelry store was going out of business—60% off! I looked in every jewelry case and found the perfect ring for me. It was gold with a cluster of small diamonds which looked like a rose in full bloom. It was a simple, low-profile setting—screaming, *"Take Me Home!"*

I was sooooo excited to show Bernie, only to find that he was disappointed because he wanted me to have a ring with a larger stone. I let him know that the size of the stone didn't matter to me as much as finding something simple yet elegant, which is what I found. Then he asked what it cost. When I told him, he replied, *"I can't afford that."* What was he thinking? A bigger stone would have been four times as expensive. Gosh, I really thought he'd be happy that I bought a ring I liked and was proud to wear—I was so hurt. I suggested that if he sold some of his clutter, he'd have the money to contribute in no time, but he didn't do it. This part of Bernie's thinking was a mystery to me. I chose to forgive him and let it go.

The result of his need to be of service to others, his joy at getting a bargain, the opportunity to make extra money, and his obvious resistance to releasing anything, meant there was no space left for me to relax or enjoy our home.

The apartment was jam-packed. A huge pile of empty boxes; four desks; two glass display cabinets; multiple printers; computer parts and cords; six 4-drawer file cabinets filled with paperwork and odds & ends; six fans both stand-up and floor; five space-heaters; hundreds of VHS tapes, CDs and DVDs; eight overflowing bookcases and 20 boxes of books of every description; numerous binders holding multi-volume self-help and money-making courses; a myriad of small kitchen appliances and gadgets—some working some broken; old cans of paint; lots of light bulbs; collections of gemstones, jewelry, minerals, stamps, coins, artwork, vinyl records, and beer steins; Christmas ornaments, lights, wrapping paper, bows, and a nativity set.

Our living room contained two large entertainment centers; three stereo systems; four big TVs; and several pieces of old oversized furniture. I could hardly get into our spare bedroom, much less convert it to the home office I really wanted.

Our driveway and side yard accommodated four cars and a van; two boats; two jet skis; two hitch trailers; and various large equipment and other items for projects never finished.

Our enormous backyard and patio, which could have been a beautiful and peaceful haven, instead was filled with a weight bench; multiple lawnmowers and weed whackers; bicycles; large kitchen appliances; uninstalled wood and tile flooring; five sheds; and an unusable swimming pool filled to the brim with broken equipment. The forty-foot semi-trailer in the RV parking space was full of tires; tools; mattresses; bedding; clothing; nick-nacks; auto parts; old license plates; sheets of glass; picture frames and matting; five tents; scads of camping equipment; ten wetsuits; a variety of snorkeling equipment; snow boards; golf clubs; and five 5-gallon buckets of used range golf balls. Last but not least, a 4-ton, dilapidated, non-functioning, above ground, fiberglass hot tub with a cement surround.

YOU NAME IT, BERNIE HAD IT—always with an intention to be useful to family, friends, and neighbors or with a plan to sell it and make more money than he had spent.

During our first couple of years living together, Bernie made little effort to release his treasures or sell the house, as he had promised before I moved in. His inaction was having a deep effect on my personal comfort and inner peace. New Year's Day 2015, during our annual intention creating discussion, I once again expressed my displeasure with the mess all around us. Also, I told him he needed to seriously step up to the plate and get rid of his clutter inside and outside our home. My suggestion was for him to create a list of things to let go of, assign priorities, and start. With a plan, the task wouldn't be so daunting. He could clear our space one area at a time, especially with my help. Well, after a while, he finally made a list. I continued to encourage him and waited—nothing happened.

By August, I was at my wits end and one evening I expressed my frustration with his lack of action. *"I work through my to do list at the office, when I come home you haven't done a single thing on your to do list. So, I add getting you to get rid of things to my list—and it's not even my stuff. There's no place for rest or respite. I want our home to be a sanctuary where I can relax and access my creativity. This space does not represent who I am. I'm embarrassed. Call your*

*friends to lend a hand. I need to see progress in the next three months or I'm
going to have to move out."*

Bernie told me he knew he needed to start and that he wanted me to be
comfortable and happy in our home, but there was so much, he didn't know
where to begin. I reminded him I would support him along with his friends
and that I was simply not comfortable inviting anyone over, because of the
clutter. He said he'd heard and understood what I needed him to do.

By Thanksgiving, I still had seen no progress, nothing was being done.
I started looking for a place to rent. It just so happened, another tenant in
my office complex, told me her mother had a fully furnished casita available
nearby—I secured it right then and there!

I arranged with a few friends to move me on December 1. On the
Saturday before I moved, I sat down with Bernie and told him, *"I'm moving
in two days. I've given you three months to show some progress and not much
has been done. I cannot stand the clutter any longer."*

*"What do you mean you're moving out Tuesday? I didn't think you were
serious."*

*"Well, I am serious. I haven't been happy living in this space. There's no
room in my mind to even think while I'm here. You haven't made much effort
or reached out to get support from me or others. I just can't be here anymore.
You spend your evenings playing poker on the internet and watching movies
when you could be releasing your stuff. Perhaps with me gone, you'll buckle
down and show some progress."*

"Where are you moving? Who's helping you move?"

*"I found a furnished one-bedroom casita, close to the office, and my friends
and I are taking my stuff over there."*

Because the new place was furnished, the move was pretty simple and
I was totally settled in by the weekend. With a place for everything, and
everything in its place—it was heavenly. No clutter, no having to clear a path
to do laundry, no wondering where I could put my things. It was perfect for
me to breathe, regroup, and think, and that's what I did.

Three weeks later Bernie and I met for dinner. He said he missed me and that he was letting go of some of his *treasures*. Bulk trash was coming up in two weeks which he planned to take advantage of, and Robert was working with him to get it done. I told him I missed him as well and was glad he had started. Yet, it hurt and upset me that it took me leaving to set a fire under his butt. What's up with that?

We began spending time together on the weekends. In hindsight, I realized he wasn't motivated to do more clearing and releasing because I was available to him again. While living away from Bernie, I came to understand that being with him was more important to me than having a clear space. When my lease was up at the end of May, I moved back in—love won out.

There was a bit of improvement, but less than I had hoped. We worked on the main house clutter and over time, it was livable, but the spare room and the apartment, were both still floor to ceiling junk! Not to mention the stacked up junk in the backyard. What's a girl to do?

I eventually established a rule—if you bring something in, you need to take something out. It worked for a little while, then one day I found a pile of Goodwill bags filled with odds and ends. I took the bags and plopped them in front of Bernie, asking, *"What is this stuff?"* He started in with his reasons and excuses, none of which I bought. Then he admitted, he was so devastated when his wife of fifteen years asked for a divorce that he needed lots of things around him as a way of surrounding himself with love and to feel prosperous. I reminded him that I loved him, and he had ME, the best deal in town right here, and he ought to spend more time nurturing what he had. He never really got it—although he made up for it in many other ways.

Bernie was always willing to help anyone with anything—often before working on projects he had committed to completing for himself or me. He was like the cobbler whose children had no shoes. I sometimes reminded him of the flight attendant's instructions, to put your oxygen mask on before assisting your children. The message to work on his projects first, never quite sank in.

Some of the most profound moments of our relationship were when our eyes met, unexpectedly. I'll never forget the time we were in a ten-seater airplane flying over the Grand Canyon. Because of the weight distribution needed, Bernie was in the back of the plane, and I was in the front. There was one miraculous moment when the beauty of the Canyon got to both of us at the same time. I turned around to look at him and he was already looking at me—we both had liquid love streaming down our faces. The experience was so intense it made a permanent mark on my soul.

Many times, we professed our feelings for each other through poetry. On Valentine's Day, 2009, I found this fantastic poem and framed it for Bernie.

My Commitment

*I promise
to trust you enough to tell you the truth
and to treat you LOVINGLY, gently,
and with respect in my thoughts, words,
and actions—whether in your presence or not.*

*In every interaction
I will surrender to LOVE, our true nature.
Being connected to God and my relationship with you
will always be more important than any issue.*

*If anything unlike LOVE comes up
I will hold us in my heart as we speak, experience,
and be RESPONSE-ABLE for our realities.*

*I will be there, for and with you,
keep communication open, and keep
LOVE conscious, active, and present—AS WE HEAL.*

~ Unknown

"I LOVE YOU," Victoria

Bernie gave me this beautiful poem he penned in May 2014. It took my breath away.

Victoria

*You are the energy, the power, the truth,
the commitment, the passion of life.*

You are always there in your greatness.

You are special and a blessing to me.

*The loving energy that you are is a feeling of peace
that comes over me.*

Your laughter surrounds me, your love is ever present.

You share your awesomeness and magnificent self with me.

*Together as we experience the deepest love,
we are both amazed, enchanted, and totally thrilled.*

The love we share is greater than anything we have ever seen.

Bold is your nature and love is your song.

*I feel your love surrounding me, encompassing all,
knowing the angel that you are will always be here.*

*The constant feeling of love that I have keeps my heart open and
patient, and my soul loving as your love is always within me.*

~ Bernie

My birthday always gave Bernie a chance to compose a heartfelt poem for my special day. The following are a few examples.

Happy Birthday Victoria

As the ocean waves come in, one at a time,
so is my love for you, one wave after the next.

The only thing there really is, is LOVE
and the love I have for you is like the ocean, limitless.

I am honored and blessed to have the privilege
to know you and to share my love with you.

May our love be enough to heal our hurts and pains,
past and present, and that we have the privilege
and opportunity to spend many more years together.

~ Your Beloved Bernie

Happy Birthday Sweetheart

Your birthday marks another year together.
Such happy times, I couldn't ask for more.
Spending precious minutes, hours, and days
With you, my love, whom I cherish and adore.

We've shared so much, we two, in love and friendship.
Each year our bond just seems to grow and grow.
I always want to be right next to you,
To be with you means more than you know.

You're always there for me with a loving smile,
I'm never happier than when I know you're near.
I thought my love for you could not grow stronger,
And yet I love you even more this year.

"With deepest love," ~ Bernie

It's Your Birthday

It's your birthday,
But I'm the lucky man, who got to be with you for another year.

It's your birthday,
And the older you get, the more wonderful you become.

It's your birthday,
And I'm privileged to share the years with you.

It's your birthday,
And each year I find the depth of my love for you growing.

It's your birthday,
And I look forward with joy to each day we spend together.

It's your birthday,
And I wonder how I got along for all the birthdays I didn't know you.

It's your birthday,
And it's amazing how easy and enjoyable it is to be with you each day.

It's your birthday,
And no matter what fate has in store for us
I know it will be a pleasure to spend life with you.

It's your birthday,
But I got the gift—you in my life for another year.

Xoxoxoxoxo Bernie

The expression of our unbridled love deepened each passing year making it easy to say, YES, to sharing another spectacular, memorable, adventurous year as Partners in Love and Life. To celebrate and create our new future, every year on our anniversary, we reflected on our relationship and made plans to renew our vows in different romantic, beautiful, sometimes tropical destinations—Las Vegas, Phoenix, Belize, and Kauai.

I could have let Bernie's lack of action and broken promises regarding clearing out his clutter and getting his house in order be my ticket out, but I would have missed out on another year of many incredible moments and the most magnificent love I have ever experienced.

Part 2

Year of the Unexpecteded

Bernie and I began 2017 as usual, by powerfully creating our intentions for the year—not knowing what was in store for each of us.

Bernie's intentions included making a difference in the world, creating his house as a beautiful sanctuary, connecting deeper in his relationships, and being a whole and complete expression of love. My intentions included making a difference in the lives of others, expanding my capacity for compassion and generosity, deepening my relationship with my Beloved Bernie, strengthening my connection with friends, clients, and family members, publishing my first book and having it reach #1 on Amazon. We brainstormed about the support and resources we would need to accomplish these goals. I then did a repatterning session so we would both resonate with realizing our intentions. Life was good!

My transformational healing practice was thriving with more and more clients each week. I established my Extraordinary Outcomes Publishing company to self-publish my books—I had seven in the queue, four self-improvement and three fiction. Working diligently on getting my first book ready for publication, I spent most Fridays and Saturdays with my editor, Paula Hofmeister, and my graphic designer, Betsy McGrew. When I wasn't working, I was spending time with Bernie, dancing, or out with my girlfriends.

Bernie continued exploring his spirituality, along with playing plenty of golf and poker, working, and spending time with his buddies, especially Robert.

One Sunday in January, Bernie and I took our regular drive to see my mom in Mesa, about an hour away. She was an incredibly independent woman and a creative cook who always prepared amazing meals—we left stuffed every time! During this visit, we noticed some memory impairment and lack of tidiness in her home, which I had never seen before—note to self.

January came and went. To me, the month of January always seems to vanish. Maybe it's because when I focus on fulfilling my intentions and doing what I love, time disappears.

My favorite holiday is Valentine's Day. Bernie would always plan something special for us to do. This year, he took me to a restaurant he knew I loved, the Phoenix City Grill. It was great seeing so many couples celebrating their love for one another.

Upon arriving home my beloved surprised me with a huge one-foot by two-foot card, professing his love for me, which filled my love tank to overflowing! He also gave me an animated, sixteen-inch, bright red stuffed bear, dressed up like a sexy devil—when I pushed the button on the bear's paw, it played *Hot Blooded©* by Foreigner.

> *Well, I'm hot blooded, check it and see*
> *I got a fever of a hundred and three*
> *Come on baby, do you do more than dance?*
> *I'm hot blooded, I'm hot blooded…*

While the music plays, images of *"I Love You," "You're the Greatest,"* and a circle of hearts appear from the devil's spinning three-pronged pitchfork. It was, and still is, hilarious to me! We didn't know this would be our last Valentine's Day together.

In 2010, I spotted a growth the size of a cherry tomato on the inside, of Bernie's left ankle. I mentioned it to him, and he said he'd have someone look at it. It slowly grew over the years. Every year I suggested again that he have it examined. Each time he'd respond with, *"I'll take care of it."* Once I asked why he was delaying getting it removed and what was frightening him. He never was able to answer me.

Three years later, he went to his primary care physician, who suspected it was a fatty tumor, and ordered an MRI. When Bernie called to schedule it, he decided that two weeks was too long to wait and didn't bother making an appointment.

The tumor continued to grow every year, so much so that by 2017 it was the size of a small orange and he could hardly wear his sandals. I often suggested that he have a specialist check it out and Robert asked him why he wasn't taking care of it. He finally researched specialists in Phoenix and found Dr. William Jacobsen—a well-known wound specialist and plastic surgeon at Abrazo Arrowhead Hospital.

Surprisingly, Dr. Jacobsen's schedule allowed us to act immediately and we set an appointment within a week, which was encouraging. During the appointment on April 5, the doctor recommended surgery for the following day, letting us know that Bernie would be in the hospital for a while afterward.

Following the surgery, the doctor told us he had removed as much of the tumor as possible without affecting Bernie's veins and arteries and used a skin graft from his thigh to cover where the tumor had been. Having to wait two days for the results of the biopsy was agonizing.

Bernie had convinced me it was just a fatty tumor, so when Dr. Jacobsen told us the result was sarcoma—one of the most aggressive, invasive, and deadliest of all cancers—I was stunned, numb with shock, and could hardly breathe!

Dr. Jacobsen also let us know it was likely that cancer cells were still under the skin graft. HOLY SHIT. In seconds, it felt like all the blood had run out the bottom of my feet. After a few moments, I realized I was furious that Bernie hadn't taken care of this tumor earlier, and distraught over the potential outcome—his death!

My plan had been to spend the next thirty years with my beloved—it was inconceivable that this wasn't God's plan for him, or for us.

Dr. Jacobsen recommended amputation below the knee ASAP, so the cancer would have less of a chance to metastasize.

Bernie explicitly stated, *"Absolutely not!"*

I asked, *"How soon can he have it done—today? Let's get him prepped for surgery!"*

We were clearly at opposite ends of the spectrum.

Bernie firmly stated, *"I want to do research first."*

"Research? Every moment counts."

I felt like hitting him over the head with a 2 x 4. Restraining myself, I opted simply to remind him that the longer he waited, the less time we would have to love each other and live our wonderful life. I assumed Bernie was in shock and couldn't fully comprehend how serious the situation was and that he needed to take action, NOW! Dr. Jacobsen even had an amputee with a prosthesis come talk to Bernie before they discharged him. Since the PET scan did not show signs of metastasis, Bernie was still adamant—NO AMPUTATION!

My online research revealed that, according to Memorial Sloan Kettering Cancer Center, there could be undetected metastasis that didn't show up because of the limitations of PET scans. When I told Bernie, it made no difference—he was hell bent on curing himself. What was he thinking? Why would he risk even one more moment without me by not taking action? I was confused—he loved me, so why wouldn't he do everything he could to stay alive? Was he afraid? He said he wasn't. Didn't he know I'd rather have him alive with one leg than not at all? I told him he had my full support in doing whatever it took for us to get through the process together.

Maintaining my personal regimen of regular activities to support my physical, mental, emotional, and spiritual well-being now became essential as things progressed.

Bernie took a medical leave of absence from his job without pay and applied for Social Security Disability, which took four months to process. This put added stress on me because I was paying all the bills, rather than my normal contribution. I did it willingly, so Bernie could focus on getting better.

When Bernie came home from the hospital, Robert drove down from Prescott Valley to stay with us for six weeks—luckily he was retired and had the freedom to make this commitment. I could go back to working with clients because he was there for Bernie. What a blessing! The key to Bernie's personal evolution was his long-time friendship with Robert. They had many conversations about Bernie's life, death, beliefs, behaviors, and why he was holding on to so much useless stuff. They also discussed the state of his relationships, especially with his father, his former wife, and their sons. Bernie began to consider the effect his words and actions, or lack thereof, had on the people in his life.

Bernie was still not ready to accept that amputation was the answer. Instead, he followed the regimen Robert used to cure himself of prostate cancer—supplements, diet, and faith. Robert joined him in researching every non-invasive alternative treatment for cancer available.

Bernie experimented with multiple food regimens—starting with a strict no-sugar diet, that he rigorously maintained throughout. He combined that with a variety of other eating plans like vegan; keto; vegetarian; liquid protein shakes; and even the Master Cleanse. Then supplements were added to the mix. He must have taken 50 varieties. All this, along with coffee enemas, CBD oil—you name it, he tried it!

At the beginning of May, Christopher started giving Bernie intravenous ozone therapy treatments. A common belief is that cancer can't live in an oxygenated environment. Therefore, having more oxygen in your bloodstream slows the growth and spread of tumors. He drove an hour each way, every day, for six weeks. What a friend! Bernie spoke of the many rich conversations they had on a variety of topics—love, life, health, travel, and spirituality.

I was uneasy, yet supportive, of all the curative approaches Bernie tried. Occasionally, I reminded him his doctor told us that sarcoma was a very aggressive cancer, and that I agreed with the recommended amputation to give him a better chance of survival. Defying the doctor's advice, he relentlessly scoured the internet and was hell bent on finding an alternative cure on his own.

One day I was looking for some documents that Bernie needed and ran across the contract for the vacation rental trial we purchased in 2015. I had talked about scheduling this trip for several months last year—Bernie's response was always, *"Not now."* Eventually, I stopped asking and forgot about it. The deadline was June 1, 2017—it was now the beginning of May. Yikes stripes! Bernie was recovering from surgery and there was no way he could travel. I made a plan to take advantage of the vacation package and go by myself, rather than wasting it.

I noticed Bernie had been losing weight. I was glad Robert was staying with us and knew he would support Bernie in his post-surgical care while I was gone. Besides organizing my travel and clearing my client schedule, I had to arrange for my sister, Denise, to fly in from Wisconsin. Our mom was scheduled for breast surgery the day before I was leaving, and she needed someone to be with her during her recovery.

Puerto Vallarta Here I Come.

I booked my stay at the Sheraton Buganvilias Resort from May 20 to June 3—two glorious weeks alone, right on the beach. I'd never taken a vacation by myself—what an opportunity to create a grand adventure.

It began with me flying standby out of the country all on my own, which I'd never done before. Lucky me, I got a first-class seat! I sat next to a woman who was an ultrasound technician. It brought back good memories of my previous medical career. We both had German husbands giving us a lot to talk about during the short flight. On my way out of the airport, a tour guide handed me a shot of tequila—feeling good!

I took a shuttle to the resort, checked in and, of course, more tequila—feeling totally relaxed! With two shots of tequila flowing through my veins, I needed food, now. Luckily, there was a fresh salsa bar in the lobby. It was sooo good!

I had the perfect studio suite on the fourth floor with a breathtaking ocean view from my balcony. There was a small kitchenette with a two-burner stove as well as a fully furnished great room. The room also included a king-size bed and a writing area next to the sliding door. I unpacked and settled in for a relaxing vacation.

I ventured downstairs and the hotel concierge told me that the nearest grocery store was only two blocks away. How cool was that? I walked to the Mega Market with confidence, even though being in a completely unfamiliar environment and not knowing the language was a little scary. I felt so proud of myself once I got there.

Naturally, everything was labeled in Spanish, so a couple of times I had to find someone to help me translate. All the local people I met during my trip had hearts of gold—willing to help me at every turn. I bought the essentials: coffee; water; produce; and meat—way more food than I could carry. At home, I was used to putting my groceries into my trunk from the grocery cart—not this time however. My backpack was full and both hands were carrying two bags each—great for my upper body workout. I was so glad I only had two blocks to walk back to the resort. I stopped a lot to rest my arms and laughed each time.

After I unpacked my groceries, I put on my swimsuit and took a long walk on the resort's beach. My Arizona skin was taking in all the ions and moisture and was exceptionally happy! The Gulf was calm and inviting—not blue like the Caribbean—but water just the same. While enjoying my walk, I witnessed a wedding, which was a splendid reminder of my ceremony with Bernie. My heart was overflowing with love for him, wishing he were here with me.

When I returned to my room, I called Bernie to let him know the flight was smooth and I was safe. He was glad to hear from me. I made myself some dinner and watched my first spectacular sunset in Puerto Vallarta. Then, I was entertained all evening by the spirited music from the wedding reception.

The second night, I tried calling Bernie and discovered that the phone plan he arranged for me was no longer working— Yikes! I had no idea what to do, so all I could do was wait for Bernie to contact me.

I spent my days in a wonderful, relaxed routine. Getting up around 8:00, in plenty of time for yoga on the beach or water aerobics at 9:00. Afterward, I'd make myself a delicious breakfast, then go down to the pool. Every day I did a little swimming, enjoyed the jacuzzi, and lounged in the shade to read. I love mystery novels and now had some time to indulge in two suspenseful books that I could hardly put down. The resort offered Spanish lessons daily. I went a few times—the 20-something instructors were talented and hilarious. All of it took my mind off my concerns about the future.

During the afternoons, I was inspired to work on the two fiction books I had written about a young girl's encounters with the Fairy Realm. Each day, without missing a beat, I did additions and revision from noon until about 5:00. It felt so natural for me to be writing and editing again—it was my favorite part of the day.

I created delicious dinners, just for me, with the healthy and flavorful food I bought at the market. The produce was fresh and nummy, the meat was tender and juicy, and the bacon was out of this world. After dinner, I played solitaire, watched a movie, or listened to some music.

Did I mention the sunsets were spectacular? Each evening around 9:00, the resort had a dazzling fireworks display that I enjoyed from my balcony. Then, I went to bed around 10:30. It felt so good to relax without distractions and excessive worry.

I wasn't interested in going into town or seeking any adventure away from the resort. Walking to the market every few days was an adventure in itself. My currency cheat sheet helped me sense how much I was spending. I always had a full backpack and at least two extra bags to carry back to the hotel.

Since the phone was nonfunctional, I started wondering about how things were going at home. By the fourth day, I really missed talking to Bernie, but I knew he was in good hands because Robert was there. I couldn't reach out to my sister, so I trusted my mom was also in good hands.

I began hearing Dr. Jacobsen's voice—loud and clear in my head—recommending a below the knee amputation ASAP to prevent metastasis. Bernie, what part of sarcoma being a highly aggressive, invasive, and deadly form of cancer, do you not understand? To me, every moment counted. What was he thinking? Although, I knew a freight train was coming sooner rather than later, I also knew I couldn't change the situation or his decision.

I took this opportunity to disconnect and allow myself to rest, relax, and rejuvenate, getting ready for what was headed our way after I got back home. What were the chances that my phone would stop working, giving me the time I needed to be alone without interruption?

On day six, I walked over to the hotel lobby and used the Wi-Fi to do some research for my books and respond to emails. That evening, I finally got a call from Bernie—he could call me, but I couldn't call him. We talked for around an hour about my trip, his recovery and ongoing research, and how we missed each other—it felt good to connect again.

By day nine, I was feeling disappointed that Bernie wasn't reaching out every day. I wondered if he was giving me my space or, frankly, just too cheap to call. I eventually figured out a way to reach him using the resort Wi-Fi, and he was delighted to hear from me and missed me a lot. He apologized for not calling me and explained that he was doing research with Robert, and he was continuing to experiment with different natural approaches to curing cancer. I reminded him that all the supplements and food plans in the world could not reverse the rapid prognosis unless they amputated and got rid of the source of the cancer so it wouldn't spread.

I asked him, "What are you waiting for? Why are you willing to risk death over life?" He didn't answer me. When we hung up, I was angry and frustrated.

Thank God I got to witness another unbelievable sunset that gave me peace for the moment. While watching the stunning fireworks, I let go of my fears and realized I couldn't control Bernie or his destiny, so I surrendered to his reality. In my heart, I committed to support him and his choices, and to refrain from telling him what I thought he should do. Accepting that Bernie's fate was in his own hands, I chose to be strong, and my internal voice let me know it all would be okay, no matter the outcome. I took a deep breath and let go some more.

On my last night, after watching the breathtaking sunset, I attended the resort fiesta and sat with a group of women I didn't know. The food was tasty, the entertainment was fabulous, and the margaritas were out of this world—what fun! It was a good thing my room was just a short walk from the festivities.

The next morning, I walked on the beach and said my goodbyes to Mother Ocean and Father Sky. Before I headed to the airport, I said farewell to the staff I'd met and gave them each a tip, which they appreciated. I arranged for a cab, packed up my things, and away I went. I arrived safely and happily, getting a standby seat on my intended flight. Yay!

During the month after Bernie's surgery and diagnosis, I had understandably spent a lot of time and energy supporting his well-being. This trip had been a wonderful chance to chill and take care of me. I was proud of the fact that I gave myself the much needed time off from everyday distractions. Because the arrangements Bernie made for using my phone never worked, I didn't talk to anyone else from home during my stay. Only twice during the whole two weeks did I check my emails. It was delightful! It surprised me that by the end of my vacation, I had read two novels and made considerable headway on revising two books.

Traveling to Mexico on my own without a confirmed seat on a specific flight had been a novel experience—my first vacation alone, and I knew it wouldn't be my last. I took all the beauty, tranquility, and revitalization of my vacation home with me—what a trip of a lifetime!

When I got home, I was immediately struck by how much weight Bernie had lost in only two weeks. Being in his arms again, sharing about our time apart and just being with each other was comforting and gratifying. We held every moment as sacred. Robert had taken such good care of my beloved that he will forever be one of my heroes!

As for my mom, it was perfect that I was unaware of what was going on while I was gone. On the second day my sister was there, my mother informed her that she didn't need any help. Then she threw my sister's things out the front door and told her to never come back. My mother's behavior seemed out of character, and I can't imagine how Denise felt. My sister called Bernie—he and Robert drove right over. She was sitting on the porch steps surrounded by her stuff, obviously in distress. They gathered her up and took her home. She stayed with them for a couple of days and then returned to Wisconsin early.

Bernie was desperate for a cure and knew he didn't have the money to pursue all the holistic options. He thought for sure his German health insurance would cover all the alternative treatments he wanted to try. Leaving the country for a month or two would risk any benefits he had achieved so far, especially if the intravenous ozone protocol wasn't available in Germany. I supported his choice, so we packed up and off we went.

> *Bernie's brother picked us up at the Munich airport and we rode three hours to visit his family in Neuenmarkt. We spent as much time as possible with his brothers and their families, enjoying their company with fresh food and awesome beer! While we were there, we got to celebrate his father's ninetieth birthday. The party was a hoot—they roasted a whole pig. I stayed from June 12 to 25, and Bernie stayed another six weeks.*

Bernie spent considerable time arranging for treatment with his primary doctor in town and an oncologist in Munich. He found out that his insurance didn't cover anything he expected it would. Germany is known for its high caliber of natural healing remedies, yet not even ozone therapy, acupuncture, or homeopathy was covered. He was so frustrated and disappointed, but he kept trying.

While in Munich for an appointment with his oncologist, Bernie took advantage of contacting Hans, a friend he hadn't seen in thirty years. They got together and spent a few hours catching up and talking about Bernie's health in the waiting room before he saw the doctor. Bernie had been hoping for a completely different treatment plan, but no such luck. The oncologist's verdict was amputation—ASAP!

A week before Bernie was due to return home, he healed his relationship with his father. They had been at odds since Bernie left the Catholic Church, joined the Unification

Church, and moved to America when he was twenty. He was the middle son of three and a free spirit bound by none—the black sheep living to the beat of his own drum. I loved that about him, but his family—not so much.

Bernie apologized to his father for not being the son he hoped for—remaining a Catholic, staying in Germany, and honoring family traditions. They talked for hours—open hearted, honest, and revealing. His father forgave him. In the last week they were together, they created a bond they never had before—Bernie felt free.

Bernie returned to Phoenix on August 9. In the following months, his younger brother called a few times with their father on the phone, so they could talk and stay connected. Bernie intended to connect deeper in his relationships this year and by golly he did!

While Bernie was looking everywhere for an alternative cure, my mother's memory was deteriorating. I drove over to see her once a month— Bernie could no longer make the trip. I had been noticing an increase in her forgetfulness, though she was still mentally sharp.

My mother had always been an exceptionally active and independent woman. She moved from Milwaukee by herself at the age of 55, started her own successful massage business, and received an Associate Degree when she was 59—I was so proud of her. She taught bridge at her local senior center, went out with her girlfriends, had card parties at her home, and took part in a local hiking club. She also attended the American Association of University Women's gatherings. My mom was a real go-getter!

In June, I discovered she hadn't been entering checks in her register or opening her mail for quite a while. Therefore, she was not aware of the $900 in overdraft fees accumulated during the past year. We sat down with the credit union manager and luckily, he understood and waived the fees. At this point, it became imperative that I needed to review her finances every month, which mom resisted adamantly.

I began wondering what other things my mom was not paying attention to. Lots of questions went through my mind that I knew I couldn't ask her. Was she taking her medication correctly? Was she eating regularly? Why did she have five new phones? Was she feeding her cats? She had gotten lost at least once driving to her doctor's office. How was she getting there now? Was she even going?

On July 18, I drove to see her and celebrate my birthday. She had a mouthwatering meal waiting for me when I arrived. It was good to visit with her. We got caught up and did water aerobics at the community pool. Every birthday, I thanked her for birthing me and taking care of me when I was little. She was appreciative. During my time with her, I tried not to mention her memory issue—when I did, it only made matters worse.

Realizing that my mom's memory was impaired and her finances were in disarray, I scheduled her for a psychiatric evaluation on July 24. The result was a diagnosis of early-stage Alzheimer's disease. I then reached out to her primary care doctor and requested a referral for a social worker. My mom met with the social worker seven days later, and then refused to accept any available resources. Meals on Wheels, transportation for doctor's visits, and monthly house cleaning, was defiantly OUT OF THE QUESTION. She insisted, *"I don't need any of that. I can take care of myself and my house. Just leave me alone."* My mom's fight for maintaining her independence had begun. I had no clue what was in store for both of us.

When I spoke to the social worker, she told me the only thing that would get my mother the care and resources she needed was for me to let her fail. As long as I was helping her and she was refusing outside support, there was nothing anyone else could do. This meant that I could no longer monitor her medication, take her to the doctor, manage her finances, and shop for her groceries. Basically, she needed to take care of herself, and I needed to stop doing anything for her and let her fail. I didn't follow this advice for a while. I found it disturbing, as well as counter-intuitive to what I thought was my responsibility as a loving daughter.

August brought another PET scan for Bernie. The result was his cancer was stage 4 and had metastasized to his lungs. OMG! Reality set in quickly for me, but not for him. He still thought he could beat it through diet, supplements, and faith. What was left of the original tumor had grown rapidly under the skin graft. Dr. Jacobsen reminded Bernie again that sarcoma was one of the fastest growing cancers and amputation was his best chance. The doctor told us that Bernie needed an oncologist. We made an appointment for mid-September at the Ironwood Cancer & Research Center.

Bernie and Robert persisted in their search for an alternative cure—absolutely nothing they attempted worked. Bernie even tried a light treatment that was supposed to kill cancer cells. Unfortunately, he left the device on too long and burned his skin graft. It was ten steps backward rather than two steps forward. He had Dr. Jacobsen re-graft the wound instead of allowing the amputation. KNUCKLEHEAD!

We met with an oncologist who was professional, kind, and told it like it was, recommending amputation—ASAP—along with chemotherapy for the metastasis in his lungs. Finally, Bernie got it and agreed to have his lower leg amputated but refused the chemo. He knew he would need to count on his immune system for the amputation and didn't want to compromise it with chemo. We scheduled the surgery with Dr. Jacobsen for September 27.

After we learned that the cancer had metastasized, I knew our time was coming to an end—I just didn't know when. Bernie and I spent a lot of quality time having long talks about the outstanding times we had traveling, at channeling sessions, hanging out with friends, and just staying home—all while celebrating our love for one another. Even the frustrations somehow disappeared as we honored the love we shared.

I made sure that we visited places we loved—some we did before the amputation and some after. We spent the first weekend of September at the cabin in Breezy Pines.

We had such a good time—building fires in the fireplace, preparing scrumptious meals, reading, relaxing, and making love. We talked about whatever came to mind—including his upcoming amputation.

I shared my confusion about why he hadn't followed the doctor's advice immediately when the cancer was diagnosed— BEFORE IT SPREAD. Why didn't he have the amputation and do all he possibly could to fight for his own life and our life together?

He admitted not taking the information seriously about how fast the sarcoma could spread. He thought for sure a cure would be available in Germany, which didn't include amputation. When he realized that wouldn't happen, he acknowledged feeling defeated and staying there too long. He apologized for how bull-headed he was in not listening to my concerns for his health over the years and then not taking Dr. Jacobsen's advice right away.

Bernie then revealed many other regrets he had, including not spending more time with his sons; not making cleaning up our home a priority; having me pay for the extra heat I needed in the winter; and often putting his needs and desires before mine. I thanked him for apologizing, which lightened my frustration and warmed my heart. He thanked me for supporting him along the way and accepting his choices even when I didn't agree—it meant the world to him. He recognized his upcoming fate and wasn't afraid to die—yet still hoped for a miracle.

We also reminisced about all the good times we shared— our wonderful day trips and vacations; our golf outings and picnics; our time with friends and family; and our many precious moments. Knowing this might be our last visit to one of our favorite places, we held each other tight and cried together—savoring each cherished moment.

Over the next few weeks, the time I spent with Bernie was so special. Robert was no longer staying with us, and we were preparing for Bernie's amputation. I was there for him every step of the way. I didn't see clients for a week, so I could dedicate my time and attention to him.

Bernie had a high tolerance for pain, so when the surgical anesthesia wore off, he hardly needed any pain meds. He said it was the weirdest feeling—it felt like his leg was still there. Bernie's hospital room had a cot where I could stay with him overnight—he insisted I go home so I could get a good night's sleep. I went home, slept well, and returned in the morning. He was resting comfortably, although a bit frustrated that they wouldn't let him get out of bed yet.

After five days in the hospital, he was transferred to an in-patient rehab center for a few days to start physical therapy and learn how to move around without his left leg and foot using a knee scooter, crutches, and a wheelchair.

When Bernie left the in-patient center, I took him twice a week for three weeks to outpatient physical and occupational therapy. These sessions taught him how to do everyday activities, like cooking; going to the bathroom; getting in and out of his car and bed. They also strengthened his upper body so he could use it when he needed to lift himself up. Everyone was so kind to us.

One of my most fulfilling opportunities during this time was to be Bernie's champion. I didn't have children, and I rarely had the opportunity of putting someone else's needs before mine. This was my chance to get a taste of what that must be like. I was still working with clients and could rearrange my schedule to accommodate his doctor visits, surgeries, rehab, therapy, etc.

One of the many ways I advocated for Bernie was to find him an artificial leg. His health insurance company understandably declined to pay for a prosthesis for a patient who had a terminal diagnosis. I wanted Bernie to walk again before he died—it was up to me to make that happen.

The Limb Center was the place I hoped would have the answer. I called them and talked to the owner, Dave Sharma, about the situation and said, *"There's got to be a used leg somewhere. I don't care if it comes from China. Find my husband a leg!"* And by golly within a week, they found one.

David Banks, a certified prosthetic assistant who had an artificial limb himself, came to the house to measure Bernie for the prosthesis. When he received his leg in October, it hardly fit because another tumor was growing behind his knee, and he had lost another 40 pounds—somehow, they got it to fit. Bernie took two steps and experienced the dignity of being able to walk. Yes, mission accomplished! It was incredibly moving to see him upright again, even if only for a couple steps. My heart was so happy for him.

This was the only time Bernie wore his artificial leg. For the next six weeks, he got around using his knee-scooter or a wheelchair without too much trouble.

In the middle of October, we took a day trip to Sedona. The fall weather was crisp, and the changing colors of the leaves were stunning—reds, oranges, and yellows.

> *We stopped at the Chapel of the Holy Cross, that is built into a rock outcropping not too far from the road. The inside was peacefully silent and the view was spectacular. There was a huge metal cross above the altar, and displays of votive candles on either side that people would light to offer specific*

prayers for themselves or loved ones. Bernie and I sat close to one another in the silence and when we felt moved to, we each lit two candles. My first prayer was to have the strength and wisdom to continue to honor Bernie's choices and be there for him as he needed me. The second was that Bernie face his fate with grace, say everything he wanted to say to everyone in his life, release any concerns he had for me, and when it was time, to just let go.

When we left the chapel, we drove to the top of the mesa to take in the breathtaking panorama of the valley. We then went to the Sedona Airport restaurant for a delicious lunch while enjoying yet another fabulous view of the stunning red rocks. This is a sacred memory that I will treasure forever.

Our last stop was at a picnic area at the lower end of Oak Creek Canyon—Bernie always found the most secluded areas. We sat and listened to the river rush by, cherishing every moment—it was serene and magical. We were quiet and peaceful during the drive home. Our time together on this trip was precious—it was our final visit to Sedona.

Something Bernie never expected happened on October 21. Bernie's youngest son and his girlfriend were spending the evening with us. As we were getting ready to watch a movie after dinner, the doorbell rang. When I answered the door, Bernie's eldest son was standing there. We welcomed him in—hellos and hugs all around. He asked if he could talk to Bernie alone, so they disappeared into his bedroom. About an hour later, they both came out holding hands with their eyes red from crying—we could feel the love between them. Another healing! They were estranged for several years, only seeing each other on holidays. I knew deep inside Bernie wanted this reconciliation as he was contemplating his remaining time on planet earth. I believe this experience allowed Bernie's son to be present for his father at the end of his life. What a miracle!

The next day, it occurred to me how great it would be for Bernie to know in his heart of hearts the immense impact he had made with the people in his life. He was always interested, caring, and engaged in what was happening for other people, and would help anyone with anything if he could.

Why get together after someone passes and talk about how much you appreciated them? Why not do so while they're alive? This prompted me to create a *Celebrate Life with Bernie* event—a perfect way for him to receive the acknowledgement he so richly deserved. It would be an opportunity for family and friends to express the difference he made in their lives.

Since most of my time was now spent in my new caretaker role, I didn't have the bandwidth to do everything that was needed for the event to happen. Without hesitation, my friend Linda, who lived about five minutes from us, agreed to host it at her home. I created an Evite event for October 29, only one week away. I gave up my need to organize the food down to the last detail, and just let everyone know it was a potluck and to bring their favorite dish to share.

Linda took the lead and, with the help of our friends, it was all done in time. They got extra chairs, made sure beverages were available, and had plenty of paper plates, plastic ware, and napkins on hand.

While others were busily managing the event, I concentrated on arranging for a Gong Meditation, creating beautiful posterboards for guests to write their comments, and making sure Bernie got to the celebration being given in his honor.

It brought me much joy to take the time to decorate two posterboards, each titled, *How Bernie Made a Difference in My Life.* One was yellow with decorative ribbon along both sides, the other was blue with a strip of gold ribbon at the top, decorated with little hearts and sequins. There was plenty of room for people to write their thoughts and feelings about how Bernie had touched their lives.

My wonderful girlfriend, Rudrani, drove over from Albuquerque the day before the event, and joined Linda, Robert, Bernie, and I for a final planning session over dinner. I wanted my mom to be there. Her dementia was worsening, and I didn't trust her to drive to my house without getting lost. Christopher, who lived near her, offered to pick her up and drive her home. Thank you, Christopher! Knowing I would need to go over to Linda's early, I arranged for Robert and Christopher to bring Bernie to his own party on time.

Shortly after Christopher and my mother got to the house, I went to Linda's to meet with Jim, the Gong Master, so he could set up before the guests arrived. As I was leaving home, I noticed everyone was searching for Bernie's teeth, which were missing in action. I wished them luck—I was counting on them to get him there. At the last minute, they found his teeth under the covers in his bed. With four of them in two cars, they all arrived at Linda's with time to spare to make sure Bernie was comfortable and we were ready to begin the celebration.

Incredibly, more than thirty-five people gathered to honor my Beloved Bernie—standing room only. He sat in a comfortable recliner thin and gaunt, having lost 80 pounds and without his prosthesis. So vulnerable and so humble at the same time. That alone was inspirational.

I wanted everyone to share how Bernie had influenced their lives. Bernie wanted no such thing. He wanted the people who were there to tell an uplifting story about their own lives so everyone could leave inspired. I began the celebration by welcoming everyone and reciting an inspirational poem.

I Celebrate Me©

I am worth celebrating. I am worth everything. I am unique.
In this world, there is only one me.
There is no one person with my talents, experiences and gifts.
No one may take my place.
I have immense potential to love, care, create, grow and sacrifice,
if I believe in myself.
It doesn't matter my age, or color, or whether my parents loved me or not.
(Maybe they wanted to, but couldn't.)
It doesn't matter what I have been, the things I've done, mistakes I've made,
or people I've hurt. I am forgiven.
I am accepted. I am okay. I am loved in spite of everything.
So, I love myself and nourish seeds within me.
I celebrate me. I begin now. I start anew.
I give myself a new birth today.
I am me, and that's all I need to be.
Today is a new beginning, a new life, given freely.
So, I celebrate the miracle, and celebrate me.
~ Anonymous

"*Who is me?*" one guest asked.

Bernie replied, "*You, everyone of you here. This celebration is not about me, it's about every one of us. We are celebrating because we're all unique individuals. We are all special, one of a kind, and sometimes we don't get this feeling because we have too much stuff going on in our head. What I would like, if possible, is for whoever wants to share, to give one short story from your life that was deeply meaningful. Go to a moment that really goes down to the guts, beyond your imagination, to an experience of love or experience of kindness. Whatever it is.*

I would like for several people to share something so we can hear what's happening in your lives and how you handled it. It's really not about me. If I'm here or I'm not, life goes on; nobody's dying. It's just a continuation of energy, of the endless love of the universe. Sometimes we think we are in control, but we are not. What happens and what will happen is up to something much greater than ourselves.

It's tough because our ego plays a pretty powerful role, and we really think we are it. And many times in my life, I've been on the top of the mountain. I thought I owned it all, and I conquered it all—only to find out that when I was on top of the mountain, I had to go down into the valley again.

And then we realize, oops, it's not quite the way we think it is. So, this is just a celebration, a celebration of life for everyone here, and I am honored and blessed for everyone who came to celebrate. I'm very appreciative that Linda opened her beautiful home for this gathering.

And Jim offers an incredible talent. I'm so in love with Jim and his gifts— how sound shows us the infinite possibilities using Tibetan singing bowls. He creates this amazing energy, and my intention for everybody is to set your own intention. We all have people and loved ones who are struggling and in need of love, in need of caring, and in need of healing, so please, this celebration is all about that.

It's a celebration for our families, for all the people we are with. We all need healing, everybody needs love, everybody needs great understanding. Community is the greatest thing of all and is what has me be here. We all need each other, knowingly or unknowingly. We all try to do it our own way and it's tough.

I guess I'm starting with my experience with my friends Christopher and Robert, who reached out to me, who went way beyond my comprehension, way out to help me—it's so powerful and so humbling. That is such an extraordinary experience—it really takes my breath away. I'm humbled and honored that so many wonderful people are in my life.

And so, I am whole and complete with my life. I was very fortunate to heal my relationships with all the people I think I've hurt in my life and to ask for forgiveness. Whatever happens, happens. I'm honored that I have the opportunity to be right here, right now.

I don't believe in a funeral kind of thing if that ever should need to happen. As long as we are here, let's celebrate life and share what we have right here and right now in friendship and in community. There are so many beautiful individuals here.

We all have so much love and kindness to share, and many wonderful things to give. Miracles happen every day and I believe in miracles. And, whatever happens, happens—I totally surrender to whatever is. It's been an experience way beyond what I could ever imagine. Wow! You know you live an okay kind of life. You try to do the right thing to help others out, and everything is good and goes well—then all of a sudden, a big wind comes.

You're in a tough situation and the questions come. Don't go to the questions, it'll drive you nuts. You can't. This is something I realized too, this universe is so incredible, so limitless, so expansive and we are the smallest denominator in the universe. Human beings are so closed-minded we can't even adapt our spiritual self to the fullest extent trying to figure it out. Wow! I've been doing this for 40 years with some success and some understanding, but the bottom line really is, it just doesn't happen, so you do the best you can and enjoy what you do. It's a journey. That's just the way it goes. And it's been a wonderful, wonderful experience.

So, I'd like to share and be the first one to tell my little story. We all have those certain songs, those certain experiences that go right to the heart. For me, it's whenever I hear the song I first heard in the 70s—**I Want to Know What Love Is**©, by Foreigner. The experience was so intense and powerful—I always wanted to know in the deepest sense what love is. I got married, had children, and experienced love to the fullest, even though that marriage didn't *quite work out.*

I have been greatly blessed to find Victoria. It was very early in our relationship that this song came to me, and I had an even fuller experience in my life to understand what love really is. It was actually at that point I said, okay, I am whole and complete. I kind of felt that one of my purposes was to have the experience of what love is and I experienced it with Victoria to the fullest extreme—spiritually and physically—and it's been absolutely extraordinary. So that means everything to me, and then, of course, we went on for many more years and had many more extraordinary experiences. It's been a wonderful life, yet I wasn't quite ready for where I am today. So, as they always say, live your life fully today—you don't know what may happen tomorrow or any other time.

I have a very good friend here, Michael, who was in an incredibly tragic accident—we all prayed for him and supported him. It takes years to fully recover from a very serious accident, and with God's blessings, he is here back to almost normal, which was very questionable at the time.

So, to celebrate life, I ask Spirit to bless every one of us here—all your family, all your friends, all your loved ones. I'm really honored that Victoria's mom is here. We got to know each other a little bit over time, and she took the time to come here and it's nice to celebrate and enjoy life with her. Whatever happens, happens. I am honored and blessed.

Thank you for coming. It's such a wonderful thing to be here in love. Is there anyone else who would like to share a story?"

Linda, the host, quickly rejected Bernie's theme of everyone sharing an inspirational story from their own lives. She said, *"Bernie, I know you don't want this to be about you, but it's all about you."* She shared about the impact he had on her life as a friend, and how helpful he had been, especially on the many occasions he fixed things around her house—like when the sprinkler system stopped working.

Person after person shared the difference Bernie had made in their life. He had so much energy that evening, unlike most of the evenings at home—it was beautiful to see. Once in a while, he requested that someone share about someone or something that had a positive impact on them. Then, Bernie explained how everyone could use the person's example in their own life. Bernie's youngest son and his girlfriend were there—it was heartwarming to watch them take in how Bernie had influenced the lives of so many people. My mom got to express her gratitude with Bernie for making me so happy, which made her really happy, and made Bernie really, really happy.

In the recesses of my heart, I was still whirling from the special words Bernie said about me and our love. In that moment, it felt as if I were alone, yet there were people everywhere. I listened intently, took to heart all the amazing things I was hearing, and was moved to tears several times absorbing the positive difference Bernie had made with the people sharing.

Throughout the gathering, I sensed the guests knew this would be the last time they would see Bernie. It was palpable—tears were flowing. My heart was bursting for all the love in the room.

We ended the Celebration with a powerful Gong meditation, which filled Bernie with renewed strength and courage. Many people stayed after the sharing to partake of the huge spread of food, along with more conversation and wisdom from Bernie. The event was exceptionally touching and heartwarming.

My idea worked. Following my intuition was clearly the best thing to do. The next day, I read the heartfelt messages filling both posterboards to Bernie. It was breathtaking to see him deeply moved by how he positively influenced other people. I knew experiencing the difference he made to the world fulfilled one of his intentions.

Here are some of the comments. Enjoy.

> *"My dear friend Bernie, you are the greatest problem solver I know! You are an adventurer par excellence! You're the dreamer I count on, the one who instills confidence in others—a wise courageous being made of ALL LOVE. Thank you for ALL that you always share from your heart, mind, and for all the*

joy and laughter you bring to me and my husband."

"Bernie, your light and questing mind has brought such joy to my life. You have been a blessing."

"Bernie, thanks so much for your unique perspective and insightful discussion! But even more, thank you for sharing your challenges. They have helped me see my own life differently and to open my mind to possible changes as well as the release that comes with them. No matter your path, keep in touch."

"Dear Bernie, you accepted me and then I learned how to accept myself and others. Love You."

"Bernie, you've encouraged me to enjoy life to the fullest. Thank you for sharing your inquisitive nature and your love! You are amazing and a blessing to all who know you."

"Bernie, you have made a difference in the world! You light up wherever you are."

"Dad. Thank you for all the lessons of the soul you taught me growing up. It was through your lessons of love, that I became the person I am today. I love you Dad and thank you for always being there for me."

"Dear Bernie, your imprint on our lives is beyond words. Your love, light, and guidance through the years has never steered us wrong. I would like to thank you for always being there for us."

"Bernie, thank you for YOU and sharing, growing, learning together. My life has been enriched because of you. I wish you the best."

"Dearest Bernie. Thank you for being a beautiful contribution

of love and communication in this world! God is doing a great work within you. All my love and blessings."

"Being humble like you, Bernie, I have learned to be patient, strong, and to never give up. Love ya."

"Bernie, what a gift for curious conversation and stimulating my neuro-nets. I love your generous spirit, your love of life and your willingness to live life lovingly."

"Bernie, you make me smile and remind me of the joyful spirit that I am by mirroring that joy!"

"Bernie, you are the man I come home to every night who provides a safe place for me to grow and be all that I can be. I am eternally grateful for you in my life. I love you. Your beloved friend and wife."

Bernie's healings with his father and his son showed me the importance of acknowledging the richness of our relationship and releasing any lingering hurts, so we could fully express our love through his transition. We shared some upsets and regrets that we still had. We let each other talk, without interruption. If an apology was needed, it was given, and we'd ask if there was anything we could do to clean the slate. Having been pretty up front with one another throughout our relationship, there were only a few things to resolve.

Bernie apologized for not providing me with a home I could call my sacred sanctuary and for refusing to work more than two days a week, which meant always being frugal. Most important to me, was his apology for not contributing to the wedding ring I found, loved, bought, and proudly wore for the past two years.

I apologized for not being as available on the weekends as he wanted me to be while I was putting the finishing touches on my first book, and ensuring my mother was taking care of herself. Also, for judging him for all the things he was apologizing for and giving up on him a few times.

The rest was joyful reminiscing. We talked about all the things we did and fun we had over the past ten years—especially our times at the beaches we visited. We acknowledged how much we valued one another for the unique qualities we each brought to our relationship. Bernie's genuine sense of contribution and his willingness to provide what other people needed, gave me the courage to create new ways to make a difference. He told me he truly valued my understanding heart, compassionate nature, and the freedom I granted him to be himself. These conversations often created tears of joy for all the enriching experiences we shared during our years together.

The harmony we gained through our willingness to forgive the disappointments and hurts we experienced with each other, often inspired those close to us. People can heal anything through communication. It wasn't always easy, but it was always well worth it.

During the last month of Bernie's life, I experienced much joy, as well as, overwhelming frustration and aggravation.

Joy! On Thanksgiving Day, two of our friends surprised us with a fabulous holiday dinner. They spent about 20 minutes talking to Bernie and me in his room about the preciousness of life and love.

Frustration! Bernie, yet again, delayed accepting the settlement offer for an auto accident he had two years prior, until the last possible moment.

Aggravation! Rather than just being able to be with Bernie as his wife, I had to ensure his finances were in order. This was a role I didn't want or welcome because it took me away from being with him. I did my best to balance my time as his wife, time as his friend, and time as his financial manager.

Since the commitment we shared was between us, we saw no reason to have our relationship officially sanctioned. This meant now there was a lot to be done to ensure the transfer of his assets to me. The house had to be deeded to me, my name had to be added to his bank accounts, the titles for his six vehicles needed to be notarized, his will had to be completed, and some other financial assets had to be transferred to me. Time was of the essence.

On November 3, Robert came to stay with Bernie so I could attend a Social Media Retreat in Atlanta. I arrived home three days later in the early afternoon. That evening Bernie's breathing became strained—he could barely catch his breath.

It was obvious to me that the tumors in his lungs had been growing rapidly—I rushed him to the ER. A nurse wheeled him into the intake room immediately, where she took his vital signs then administered oxygen. His breathing got better, although it was still labored. They brought in the equipment to take a chest x-ray, an EKG, and draw blood. It took several hours to get the results.

While we were waiting, they transferred Bernie into an ER exam room. The doctor arrived with the test results and put the x-ray up on the light box. Before he even spoke, as a former x-ray technician, I could see that large tumors filled Bernie's lungs—tumors so big that there wasn't much space left for breathing. I knew his death was imminent. My heart sank. The doctor was kind and caring, he approached Bernie with dignity. He touched his arm as a way of expressing compassion for Bernie's fate, told him the truth, recommended we take an oxygen tank home, and arrange for hospice care.

Tumors, oxygen tanks, hospice—OMG! My world came tumbling down right in front of my eyes—confirmation that our life together was coming to an end very soon. Bernie could see I was tearing up, and he followed suit. The staff left the room to give us the time we needed to take in this new reality. We held hands for a while and then I lowered the rail on the hospital bed, leaned over, gave him a big hug, and held him for several minutes.

Bernie and I then walked up and down the halls in the emergency room until the nurse validated his need for an oxygen tank. It took about thirty minutes. They put him back on oxygen and we rested until he was stable again. They provided us with a tank to take home and told us that more breathing equipment would be delivered later. We got home at 3:00 in the morning and immediately crashed.

When I woke up, I called Hospice of the Valley and started the process for in-home care. It was a difficult and emotional call to make. Bernie's fate was inevitable—my fate was unknown. The hospice nurse and doctor recommended in-patient care so they could evaluate Bernie and his condition. When I finished the call, I broke down and cried for what I knew I was losing—the love of my life. From this point on, most of my tears, when they surfaced were pre-grieving the loss of Bernie—I was missing him already. I didn't keep my tears back when I was with him, however, my moments of weeping were usually in my bedroom right before I went to sleep, where he couldn't hear me.

Arriving at the hospice facility on Thursday, November 9, everyone was so respectful and honoring. They did everything in their power to make him comfortable. Understandably, he just wanted to go home. They let me know I could stay there overnight. I opted not to—I needed a good night's sleep in my own bed.

I knew it was important for me to take care of myself during all of this, so I could continue serving Bernie in a genuine, reliable, and loving way. The next two days, I spent most of my time with him, except for Friday morning at my acupuncture appointment and Saturday afternoon getting my regular massage at home, both of which allowed me to relax.

They released Bernie from the facility on Sunday and we switched to home hospice care. The nurse, Mikelle Swafford, made in-home visits for the first two days, then twice a week unless we needed something—she was an angel. She instructed me on how to give Bernie oral medication to keep his bronchial tubes open and to ease any pain—neither of which he used much until his last few days.

The oxygen concentrator that provided a higher absorption rate than the oxygen tank, was delivered the next day. The respiratory specialist came out to ensure I could switch the equipment from the tank to the concentrator when Bernie needed it. It was an ordeal switching between the nasal cannula and the face mask. Twice, I had to get the instructions and follow step by step, which helped me trust my ability to switch over quickly, so Bernie would never be without oxygen. Making sure it worked every time was exceedingly stressful. I needed to take a few deep breaths myself when I completed the switch. Imagine someone else's fate in your hands—breathing or not breathing. Yet, I knew in my heart, the best place for me to be was right by my sweetheart's side, providing as much love and care as possible.

The first week Bernie was back home, I took all the excess furniture and other things he wouldn't need, out of his room, so his last weeks were clutter-free and less stressful. I brought in some kitchen chairs so people could sit down when visiting. To have beautiful music available whenever he wanted, I set up his computer on the bed where he could access it on demand. He truly enjoyed, *Musical Rapture, A Healing Gift to Humanity©,* by João Costa-Robles, which we looped for his ongoing pleasure.

When visitors arrived, I gave them their time with Bernie. Often, they would request my presence, and I was glad to join them. Nothing much mattered except making sure Bernie was as comfortable as possible, and that he saw as many people as he wanted to see. Several people who could not make it to the *Celebrate Life with Bernie* gathering, came to visit.

Bernie encouraged me to do what I needed to do for myself, including seeing clients. In order to work at my office and still support Bernie, I would coordinate my schedule with Robert so he could stay with Bernie since he was the only other person who knew how to transfer the oxygen. I rearranged my calendar so that I could meet with four clients every week. The transformational healing sessions were profound, and each client appreciated and was thankful for my support. It was a pleasure to focus on someone other than Bernie or myself.

The most important thing I needed Bernie to do was settle the case to receive the insurance settlement for his auto accident. He wanted me to appeal to get more money. I told him, *"No one is going to court for a dead man. Settle the case, so I'll receive some money to pay the mortgage."*

Adding a $600 mortgage payment to my living expenses was daunting. With this insurance payout, I'd be set for almost a year. He then took action and made the necessary phone calls to get it done. On Friday, November 24, at the beginning of our last weekend together, they settled the case—just in the nick of time.

The third week of November, Bernie's friend Hans visited from Germany. I spoke with him briefly to let him know about the condition of our home and that Bernie was a treasure-hunter—finding more treasures than he was willing to release. He had promised Bernie he'd help, and HELP he did. He was a delightful, fun-loving man and a real outdoorsman. Bernie could still speak when Hans arrived so they shared many hours of deep conversations about life and love, some of which I was privy to. Hans took a spare mattress we had and created an area on our back patio so he could sleep under the stars.

It was wonderful getting to know Hans. He had an open, generous heart. We had long talks about our lives, the loves we'd been through, and how he could be most helpful to me. It was unusual for me to be on the receiving end—I was normally the one giving. Now, I had the opportunity to learn to accept support, not only from him, but from so many others.

Thanksgiving morning I received a text message from a friend inquiring about why we hadn't attended any group healing sessions recently. I told her all about Bernie's health challenge and that he was in his process of preparing to transition.

She asked, *"Do you have food for your Thanksgiving meal?"*

"No."

"Please let us bring you leftovers from our group feast."

"Sure, that would be great. Thank you."

They brought the whole kit and caboodle for a meaningful Thanksgiving dinner, visited with Bernie, gave us their blessings, and left us to enjoy the feast.

I set the table and put out the food. Through their kind offering, I created a beautiful display of my love for Bernie. I helped him out of bed and into his wheelchair with his oxygen tank, then he wheeled himself into the kitchen and sat up at the table. Even though this dinner was a joyous occasion, we both had a few tearful moments—we savored our last Thanksgiving celebration.

Our friends' gracious act of generosity prepared me to be open to the many opportunities I would have to receive food, flowers, love, and more from all the wonderful people who were there for me after Bernie transitioned.

The next day, after Bernie received word that the insurance settlement from his automobile accident was assured, he said to me, *"Victoria, after tonight, we have two more nights together."* I was too choked up to speak. We held hands and looked into each other's eyes. Tears were flowing for both of us. Our life of love, joy, fun, travel, and adventure was ending. How could this be happening? My Beloved Bernie was disappearing right in front of me. I went to my bedroom and had a good cry.

Bernie insisted that I go to Torina channeling that evening. He was still looking for answers and wanted me to ask if there was anything he could do to heal his body, or to prepare himself for the other side. They suggested he continue to love himself and focus on his contributions rather than where he thought he fell short with the people in his life.

During these final days, Bernie was deteriorating rapidly. The tumors filling his lungs made it significantly more difficult for him to breathe and talk. Being on oxygen helped a little. I knew his last breath was rushing toward us. Our remaining time together was extremely precious.

Bernie could only breathe while sitting up and leaning over, so I held him from behind for hours—I only got up to pee and eat. I read to him from, **Whatever Arises, Love That: A Love Revolution That Begins with You,** by Matt Kahn. As he could barely speak, we communicated by writing things down. We cherished each breath we still had together. I massaged his body, telling him in that way, how much he meant to me. I looked into his beautiful blue-green eyes as often as possible, as we exchanged smiles of love and honor for each other. It filled my heart to overflowing. Bernie maintained a positive attitude to the end. Hans said that Bernie even told him that he still believed a divine intervention and an instantaneous miracle could happen.

On Monday morning, my beloved was feeling more restless than usual. He needed oral doses of both medications every hour to ease his breathing and reduce any pain, which calmed him down. I realized that what Bernie had said on Friday meant—today was the day.

He continued to be agitated and showed signs of being incoherent. I was following the protocol the hospice nurse had provided and hoped I wasn't giving him too much morphine. Bernie was sitting on the lower right corner of his bed, and I spent all day by his side. His labored breathing made it hard for him to even drink water. I held him close as he sat up, slightly bending over to breathe. Knowing he was not in any pain comforted me.

I asked Bernie if he wanted Revered Tina to come over to give him some more energy healing. He nodded yes, and I made the call. We listened to his favorite inspirational music all day. As this beautiful music filled the room, it became a sacred space—we both felt more peaceful and calm.

That afternoon I called Bernie's eldest son and said, *"If you wish to be present for your father as he takes his last breath, come now. This is not the time to be late. You will either make it or you won't. You choose."* He came over around 3:30 and spent ten minutes with his dad and then left the room.

Hans went out to talk with him and was dumbfounded to find him in the kitchen playing games on his phone. Hans said, *"I know you're uncomfortable, but if you want to be there for your dad, now is the time to man up and get* back into that room. Bernie would love to have you there. If you don't, you may regret it the rest of your life. It's up to you!" He followed Hans back into the bedroom, sat down on the bed in front of his dad, and stayed present to what was happening as his father was dying.

At 3:45, Bernie whipped off the oxygen mask—I wasn't sure if he was delirious, so I simply transferred him to the nasal cannula. He took it, then five minutes later he yanked it off. I said, *"Okay Bernie, I get it's your time. You may want to have some oxygen coming in so the transition to not having oxygen will be less stressful. You choose honey."* He let me put the cannula back in his nose.

Reverend Tina arrived at 4:00, came into the bedroom, and stood to Bernie's left. We were all surrounding him in loving support. I nodded my head and told her it was his time. She started sending him healing energy.

I let Bernie know he was free to leave, to simply let go. I said, *"Everything will be fine—I'll be fine, your kids will be fine, the house will be fine."* I reminded him to look for all his family and friends waiting for him—his mother, his best friend Bernhart, and my father would all be there to greet him; and that God, Jesus, and all the angels on high were anticipating his arrival.

I wanted one more moment of eye contact with Bernie, so I bent over, looked into his gorgeous eyes one last time, smiled and said goodbye. He slightly nodded his head, squeezed my hand three times telling me, I LOVE YOU, and took his last breath at 4:15 pm Monday, November 27, 2017.

Suddenly, there was so much divine energy it was palpable—his presence and large spirit, permeated the room. The air was thick with the most powerful pristine energy I had ever felt—like all the angels in the universe were right there singing his praises. There was silence for about five minutes. Tears of ecstasy and happiness for him overcame me. He had liberated his soul from his physical body—he was free. It felt so divine; so pure and sparkly.

I was thinking about the large energy we all have that is trying to do its best inside the small vessel of our body. It reminded me how important it was to remember that we are spiritual beings having a human experience and that our essence is expansive. It also made me think about how challenging and encumbering it is sometimes to have a body as we move through life carrying out our spiritual work here.

None of us wanted to move or leave. We all held hands in remembrance of this time we shared—never to be forgotten. I am bonded forever with Tina, Hans, and Bernie's son. After a few minutes, we stretched out his body and moved him to the left side of the bed, where he slept during all the years I knew him. This was one of the most sacred experiences I've had in my life.

Rudrani shared with me the Jewish tradition called Taharah. According to this tradition, loved ones cleanse the body—so I did just that. Using a small container of warm, soapy water, I washed every inch.

I told Bernie out loud how appreciative I was to share my life with him. I honored his head containing his wonderful brain that taught me so many things in so many ways. Moving to his face and knowing the eyes are the windows of the soul, I thanked him for all the moments when our eyes met expressing our joy for the opportunity to love one another. I thanked his ears that listened attentively; his nose that breathed in life; his lips for all the kisses, and then gave him my last kiss.

I thanked his arms for the hours of embrace we shared and all the ways he used his hands to comfort me and to complete projects around the house. Next, I washed his torso and abdomen and as I washed his penis, I thanked it for the many hours of pleasure it provided me as we made love so tenderly. I thanked his legs for their strength and for all the places in the world they took us, and the foot he had left, for all the walking and hiking we did. Turning him over slightly, I washed his back, thanking his spine for the support he provided by always having my back.

It was profoundly moving to honor the body Bernie had occupied for 62 years, and to celebrate all the love we had for each other—I was on cloud nine. After I finished, I could still feel his energy in the room.

Hans then helped me dress him in his favorite Hawaiian shirt and a pair of khaki shorts. As we were putting on his shorts, I took a last look at his penis and commented, *"Wow, what a good time we had with that."* It struck both of us as hilarious and we couldn't stop laughing for a couple of minutes. Hans later told me he had witnessed me saying farewell without mourning— something he thought the world could definitely use.

I left the room so that Bernie's son, Tina, and Hans could have their time with him alone. I called his youngest son to tell him that his father had passed and let him know that if he wanted to pay his last respects I would wait for him before calling hospice—he said he did and arrived about an hour later. Then, I called Mikelle, to tell her that Bernie had died and she could contact the mortuary to pick up his body.

Even though I knew Bernie was no longer there, I went back once more to show my respect for him. I swirled my hands from his head to his toes and bowed in honor of the privilege it had been to share ten years of my precious life with him—for which I was eternally grateful. I left the room filled with the spirit of the Divine.

Bernie's sons and Reverend Tina left soon afterward. Hans offered to wait for the mortuary to pick up Bernie's body and I knew the right place for me to be was with the Higher Vibrations choir. Within minutes I was in my seat singing with the group. The spiritual nature of the people and the harmonies created, added to the sense of bliss and tranquility I needed in the moment.

Along with connecting through music, we connected through introducing ourselves. When it was my turn, I said, *"Hi, I'm Victoria, my beloved husband Bernie, who I had the privilege of being with for ten years, liberated his soul from his physical body three hours ago and I am here to sing his praises."* Silent reverence filled the room.

Whenever anyone passes we sing the song *Fly Away Home*©. According to the composer, Harold Grandstaff Moses, it's a song of remembrance and release for those who have passed from this world to the next. It simply states our desire that the departed soul separate completely and move fully into the Light of Love.

I requested we sing this song to release Bernie's soul.

> *Fly away home, Fly away home,*
> *Fly away home, Fly away home.*
> [Clap]
>
> *Fly away home, Fly away home,*
> *Fly away home, Fly away home.*
> [Clap]
>
> *Fly away home, Fly away home,*
> *Fly away home, Fly away home.*
> [Clap]
>
> *Fly away home, Fly away home,*
> *Fly away home, Fly away home.*
> [Clap]
>
> *Fly away home, Fly away home,*
> *Fly away home, Fly away home.*
> [Clap]

Again, there was a profound stillness, silence, and reverence present in the room. We sang the night away. At the close of the evening, people expressed their astonishment that I could be there with so much radiant energy when my husband just died hours ago. It was heartening to be an example of how one can experience the passing of a loved one with devotion rather than devastation.

To keep the beautiful memory of washing my beloved and saying my personal goodbye as my last image, I called Hans to make sure Bernie's body had been picked up. It hadn't, so I went grocery shopping and bought myself some flowers and a few items I needed. When I called again, Bernie was gone. I arrived home at about 9:30 and Bernie's energy was still palpable in his room. Hans and I stayed up talking for a while, then I headed for bed and had a peaceful night's sleep.

My saving grace with the loss of Bernie was that prior to his death, we had communicated all things of importance and healed our unresolved emotional wounds. For a moment or two, I questioned why I never made a doctor's appointment for Bernie and forced him to go—even if I had to use my 5'3" 120 pounds to drag his 6'3" 210 pounds there myself. However, now I know why—it was HIS TIME to transition. If he hadn't passed this way, he might have died suddenly and I wouldn't have had a chance to say goodbye, or champion him as I did. It was his choice; I came to terms with my choice and had no regrets.

I didn't have much experience with grief. I had only lost two people who were special to me prior to Bernie's passing—my close friend Jenny, and my beloved father.

Jenny died of leukemia when we were 14. She was a soft-spoken, gentle spirit with a big heart—helping anyone she could, animals in particular. She was a good listener and seemed wise for her years. I talked to her about anything and everything, including my parent's separation. Through our conversations, I saw my home situation from a different perspective, which made it easier for me to cope.

Jenny and her boyfriend were together for about a year, like two peas in a pod. Unlike the tension and animosity in my parent's marriage, I often observed their kind, caring actions and honest communication—it gave me hope for my future relationships.

To deal with my grief at the loss of my friend, I cried the first few days and then I started sending her love, telling her I missed her. Mostly, I stayed to myself and thought about all the good times we had. I also felt compassion for what her boyfriend was going through. My father helped me see that perhaps God needed her in heaven more than on earth. Although, I didn't quite grasp this, it consoled me.

Through this experience, I came to understand that death was a natural part of life, and started realizing how precious my life really was.

My father died in 2011 of metastatic lung cancer. We had a close loving relationship and talked regularly by phone. Most years I spent several days visiting him in Milwaukee. We loved canoeing on a local lake near his house, hiking, and going to the farmer's market. Spending hours looking through the family photo albums, delighted us both.

When I was visiting him shortly before he died, we knew it would be our last time together. Humbly, I told him how much I loved him and appreciated him for being my father, and that I knew being a single dad wasn't easy for him when we were little. I got all teary-eyed, and he burst into singing, ***Don't Cry for Me Argentina©*** by Andrew Lloyd Webber and Time Rice. We both cracked up laughing.

He was in so much pain from the cancer, I felt relieved when he died—he was a devout Catholic, so I knew he was with Jesus and Mary. We had communicated our love for each other and there was no unfinished business—that's all I needed.

Day One
Tuesday, November 28

I woke up a bit disoriented, walked toward Bernie's bedroom, then oops I realized he wasn't there. Reality hit me like a ton of bricks, filling my mind and body with a knowing that Bernie was gone. I walked into the kitchen to make coffee, and Hans was already there. We said good morning, sat down, and shared about the astonishing experience of being present for Bernie's liberation.

Before Bernie died, he told me he would send me a sign that he was near. As I was leaving the room, I noticed two bright shiny pennies right in the middle of the floor that I didn't recall seeing when I came in. I smiled and picked them up, it was the perfect sign from Bernie. I added them to his giant penny jar. I started seeing pennies everywhere I went—and in the oddest places. My heart filled with a warm feeling each time I found one.

Next, I called my mom and told her Bernie had died. She became very emotional, which is why I hadn't called her the evening before. I reassured her I was doing okay, that Hans was with me, and others were planning to visit later that morning. It frustrated her that she couldn't just get in her car and drive over—I did what I could to console her.

After talking to my mother, I called my siblings to let them know. They each expressed their sorrow for my loss and asked if I had the support I needed. I told them Hans was at the house and friends were already arriving. They let me know that they were available and would help if necessary. I thanked them for their love and support.

I ordered a three-ton dumpster for delivery the very next day. You may wonder, why the heck I needed a dumpster on day one? Hans had made a promise to Bernie that he would help me clean up the backyard, so we needed to begin before he had to go back home. To be ready when the dumpster arrived, we started identifying what could be thrown away immediately—which was most of it. While Hans was sorting stuff outside, I got another sign from Bernie, this time pennies in my bathroom, one on the floor and one by the sink. Another smile and more pennies into the jar.

Bernie hadn't wanted an obituary in the newspaper, or any type of funeral gathering, so I had to contact people personally to let them know of his passing. It was heartwarming to speak with the wonderful people I called, and I spent as much time as I could talking with each person. Everyone asked me what I needed, which was uncomfortable for me. I knew I didn't need the tangible things people could provide, so I wasn't always sure how to answer that question. After a while, I realized I just wanted to be with people who loved and cared about me—although the only thing I truly wanted was my Beloved Bernie back in my arms.

Several people came by to pay their respects, filling my kitchen with gorgeous flowers, heartfelt cards, and enough food to feed an army. We talked about how much they loved Bernie and the positive influence he had in their lives. I was mostly upbeat knowing Bernie was free. I felt his presence as if he were right over my shoulder listening to each conversation. Whenever a close friend stopped by, we would cry for my loss for a few minutes, and then I was back to my cheerful self. I continued to be blown away by the open-heartedness of so many people and greatly appreciated Hans' silent presence giving me the space to focus on being with each person. I felt so blessed.

It was an emotional day. There were some tears of longing for Bernie and mostly tears of joy that I shared with others about how incredible Bernie had been. The reality of him being gone was setting in.

Day Two
Wednesday, November 29

I was getting more comfortable inviting people to spend some good quality time with me. I allowed myself to receive and started welcoming everyone's generosity. Flowers, cards, and food were still flowing.

Rudrani came to stay with me for three days. She knew how important it was for me that she made herself available. I had been there for her when her husband had died suddenly while I was visiting them on my way to a conference. I gladly stayed to help her for which she was tremendously appreciative. It amazed her that I changed my plans to be with her—I wouldn't have had it any other way. Even though she was there to support me in my loss, we had a hoot. Rudrani is hilarious and kept me upbeat—we laughed, then cried, then laughed and cried some more. We enjoyed the food people had left, and she baked her world-famous brownies. Her comforting presence allowed me to begin healing.

It was so reassuring to have Rudrani by my side while I resumed making phone calls—especially during the call to Bernie's middle son who lived in Germany.

When I told him his father had died, his immediate response was, *"Did he have a will?"*

I was flabbergasted. *"That's the first thing you want to know?"* He then informed me he was flying to Phoenix as soon as possible.

Robert came over in the afternoon and was incredibly supportive. He told me he had promised Bernie he would help me clean up the yard. He started right in working with Hans filling the dumpster that had arrived around noon. When I went outside to call them in for dinner, there were more pennies by the door. More evidence Bernie was around watching over me. I couldn't stop smiling—I wondered if the pennies were jumping out of the jar.

Surrounded by friends, I still missed my beloved. Most of the tears that came were tears of joy knowing how much he loved me. That evening, I held a framed photograph of him close to my heart when I went to bed, which was enormously comforting.

Day Three
Thursday, November 30

Bernie's youngest son arrived in the morning and jumped right in with Hans and Robert filling the dumpster, while I made more phone calls and visited with people who stopped by. I called the airline where Bernie worked and talked to his supervisor, Ron, and the HR Manger, Kenneth—they both expressed their deep sadness and were of enormous assistance to me.

Ron spoke highly of Bernie, *"He was such a great man and great worker, he will be missed."* I let him know that no memorial service was planned and that he could give my phone number to any employees who wanted to offer their condolences.

He asked me if I needed to fund the cremation or any other final expenses. I mentioned Bernie had left no life insurance, and that I now had extra costs besides my regular monthly expenses. He set up a GoFundMe account to allow Bernie's co-workers to pay their respects by contributing. The account description read:

To all my brothers and sisters at Piedmont Airlines, one of our own in Phoenix, Bernie Klein, liberated his soul from his physical body on Monday, November 27, 2017. I have created this GoFundMe page so that we can raise money for his wonderful, surviving spouse to help out with final expenses and any remaining medical bills. Please help out with anything you can. Every little bit helps.

Including our friends, 65 people made generous contributions and I received over $3,000, that paid for his cremation, the property taxes, and the mortgage for the next couple of months. The outstanding generosity from so many of our friends and Bernie's co-workers who were positively affected by knowing him, moved me to tears. I told Ron how much all his kindness and support meant to me and that he was one of my heroes.

Kenneth was also a major help and another hero! He was my go-to man whenever I had questions. After I sent him a copy of the death certificate, he waived Bernie's accumulated standby charges that I knew nothing about. Next, he made sure I received Bernie's 401K funds, which paid for another month's mortgage. Then when I was ready, he was instrumental in getting me to Kauai to spread Bernie's ashes. I felt so taken care of.

Thank you Ron, Kenneth, and everyone at Piedmont. Unfortunately, Bernie was six months shy of his 10-year work anniversary, which meant I was not entitled to his lifetime travel benefits—bummer!

As I fell asleep that night, my heart was full remembering all of my great travels with Bernie and the impact he made in the lives others.

Day Four
Friday, December 1

More calls and more visitors. I definitely appreciated everyone's support.

Bernie's son and I talked briefly after he arrived from Germany—his attitude wasn't much different from what it had been on our first call. Later that day, while Rudrani and I were out running errands. He came to the house, climbed over the fence, and tried to break into my home. When he couldn't find an open window, he called me demanding to know where he could find a key. I was outraged and shouted, *"What are you thinking, that Bernie had some hidden jewels? He didn't even have life insurance. You can't come into my house when I am not there. There is no hidden key. If you're still on my property when I get back, I'll call the police and have you removed."*

When Rudrani and I got home, Bernie's son was gone. I immediately wrote an email to him expressing how violated, disrespected, and deeply hurt I was by his insensitive actions and demands. I copied the email to his mother and brothers.

In the email, I told him that I had lost all trust and respect for him. In addition—under no uncertain terms—would I let him bully or intimidate me, nor allow him access to my property or my house without my presence and permission. The email continued with me letting him know that he would be informed of the day, date, time and location of the reading of the will—AFTER I confirmed when his brothers and Robert were available. Following the reading, he would have the opportunity to go through the house to select any personal mementos he wanted.

I was so grateful that Rudrani was there with me during this upsetting situation, and Robert reminded me that everyone grieves in their own way. This allowed me to put Bernie's son's reaction into perspective and released me to continue my own grieving and mend my heart.

I healed my heart from the upsets of the day by reconciling the violation of Bernie's son, along with the hurt and betrayal I felt.

That night I attended the monthly Equinoxx channeling session. It was so odd not seeing Bernie in the chair at the front of the room where he sat every month. The evening wasn't quite the same, but I still enjoyed it. I knew it was too soon to receive a message from Bernie, so I didn't even ask.

Along with the emotional support provided by Rudrani and the people at Equinoxx, Robert's wise words also consoled me. All of this allowed me to be present to my longing to be held by Bernie—I felt his arms around me and rocked myself to sleep.

Day Five
Saturday, December 2

I received an unexpected email from Unity Church about their semi-annual remembrance service, which was scheduled for the following Tuesday evening—coincidence? They asked anyone who wanted their loved one included, to send a photograph. I found a fabulous picture of Bernie and emailed it to them.

There was some relief in seeing my backyard being cleared out, especially when the overfilled dumpster was picked up around noon. I was thankful for all the exceptional support I received clearing some of the clutter from the backyard. Yet, three tons of junk disposed of had hardly made a dent in the huge list of things yet to be cleared. It thrilled me to be able to see most of my backyard, even though the semi-truck container, all five of the sheds, the pool, and most of my patio were still packed to the gills.

Rudrani returned home in the afternoon. I was sorry to see her leave and I was so grateful for her support. Reverend Tina invited me to be her guest at a home concert that night where Robin Miller from Sedona was performing. I gladly accepted. It was great seeing old friends, some of whom did not know about Bernie's passing. The evening was filled with peaceful moments and times when I longed for him to be at my side. It reminded me once again, of the love people had for Bernie—the love I had for Bernie.

Day Six
Sunday, December 3

I attended Unity Church. It was tough—I was so used to sitting with Bernie holding hands during the service. A part of me wanted to sit alone, and another part longed to have someone come and sit with me—I sat alone.

I left quickly so no one would approach me and ask where Bernie was, I didn't have it in me to tell anyone that he had died. Attending was enough for me—I just needed to integrate the personal strength and encouragement I had received.

After church, I drove Hans to the airport to catch his flight home. Although, I hated to see him leave, I was wildly appreciative of the two weeks he had devoted to being with Bernie and starting the backyard cleanup. His physical, emotional, mental, and spiritual support during this time made a tremendous difference to me—he had kept his promise to help me and then some.

I had known that the day would come when everyone would go home, yet, I hadn't prepared for how totally alone I would be—alone in my thoughts, alone in my emotions, alone in my life. I had spent the past ten years providing love and care for Bernie, and this year prioritizing his health challenges and coming to terms with his imminent death. Who did I have to love and care for now? My answer was, ME.

When I went into my bedroom, the first thing I saw was a penny next to my bed. Fond memories of Bernie's love for me flooded my mind—I felt his presence close to me. Once again, I placed his photo on my heart and cried myself to sleep, longing for him to be physically right here with me, holding me tight.

Day Seven
Monday, December 4

Betsy came over for lunch, and we completed the preparation for my Amazon book launch in two days. Afterward, I went to my regular physical therapy appointment. That evening I took part in the Higher Vibrations choir as usual—clearing distractions, connecting with God, and centering in my heart.

I started to see that life without Bernie was possible, even though it was difficult being in my home by myself. Evidence of him was everywhere, the good and the clutter—I focused on the good times and allowed my emotions to surface when they did. Mostly, I embraced all the love we had shared, which helped me focus on moving forward.

Week Two

I resumed my regular schedule of personal and business activities, like self-care, socializing with friends, and seeing clients—I knew Bernie would be pleased. It felt so nurturing to focus my attention on my well-being.

Betsy and Paula had been instrumental in getting my book ready for publication, and it was very satisfying to give back by providing repatterning sessions to each of them. All of it helped considerably to balance my energy and keep me sane amidst all that was happening around me.

I was totally unaware of how much was involved in settling someone's estate. Bernie and I had resolved many financial and legal issues before he passed. He put my name on most of his assets and accounts, now I needed to contact them to remove his name. By working through this list one a day, or one a week, or whenever I could handle it, I achieved 99.9% of the changes within a year—I resolved the last asset two years later.

On Tuesday, I drove out to visit my mom for the first time after Bernie's death. We cried, had lunch, talked about how wonderful Bernie was, and cried some more. My mom shared how frustrated she was because she wanted to be more available to me during this time but circumstances prevented her from driving.

After lunch, I left in plenty of time to beat the traffic and attend the remembrance service at Unity Church. The whole ceremony was outstanding, and the music moved my heart. When I saw Bernie's picture up on the big screen, I cried for a few minutes, wishing he was there with me. One of the officiants came and sat with me, which warmed my heart. Here's one poem the officiant recited.

The Traveler©

He has put on invisibility.
Dear Lord, I cannot see—
But this I know, although the road ascends
And passes from my sight,
That there will be no night;
That You will take him gently by the hand
And lead him on
Along the road of life that never ends,
And he will find it is not death but dawn.
I do not doubt that You are there as here,
And You will hold him dear.
Our life did not begin with birth,
It is not of the earth;
And this that we call death, it is no more
Than an opening and closing of a door—
And in Your house how many rooms must be
Beyond this one where we rest momently.
Dear Lord, I thank You for the faith that frees,
The love that knows it cannot lose its own;
The love that, looking through the shadows, sees
That You and he and I are ever one!
~ James Dillet Freeman

On December 6, 2017, I became a published author! I did a shout-out to at least six Facebook groups and within a week, *What Would Love Do Right Now? A Guide to Living an Extraordinary Life* was a bestseller at #12 on Amazon. What a feeling!

After Bernie's death, I needed a renewal of sorts and publishing my book fit the bill. He had been so supportive during the many hours I spent revising, formatting, uploading, designing the cover, gathering testimonials, creating worksheets, and much more. I knew Bernie was so proud of my efforts and the courage it took for me to release the book, only nine days after he passed. I could tell he was smiling down on me.

Friday, I received a call from the funeral home letting me know that Bernie's ashes were ready.

When I got there, the lobby was full of people waiting for their loved one's celebration ceremony to begin—I felt like an intruder. An assistant greeted me then left and returned with the urn, which he handed to me. I burst into tears and said, *"Is this all that's left of my 6'3" Bernie? Is this all I have to remember my beloved by?"*

The assistant was so kind. He led me to a quieter part of the lobby, had me sit down and offered me some water. Then he looked me right in the eyes, told me he was sorry for my loss, and reassured me that many people have the same response, especially when it's their first time picking up someone's ashes. I took some deep breaths and finished my water, thanked him, then walked to my car, strapped Bernie into the passenger's seat, and drove home teary eyed. It mystified me that ten years of an exceptional relationship with an exceptional man could fit into such a small container.

My tears had subsided by the time I got home. I placed the urn at the center of my fireplace mantle. It would remain there until I could travel to Kauai and scatter Bernie in the ocean as he wanted—I had no clue when I was going to pull that off. Time would tell.

Saturday evening, I went to the annual Christmas party at Reverend John

Adams' house—this gathering was always a highlight of our year. Most of the people there didn't know Bernie had passed, which allowed me to share about his liberation.

Rather than attending my regular church service on Sunday, I started writing in my journal. It came to me that I wanted to capture my experiences of Bernie's passing and our life together—and so this book began. I didn't have a title, but I trusted it would come to me when I was ready.

I knew I would need copies of Bernie's death certificate, so I went to the County Vital Records Office and picked up a few. I used the first one, along with his will, to have the bank recognize me as the recipient of the accident settlement check, which was in Bernie's name. The rest of the day I spent my time having a physical therapy session, working on promoting my bestselling book, and attending Higher Vibrations choir—a much needed opportunity to soothe my heart and feed my soul.

It was hard to believe two weeks had already flown by without my Beloved Bernie. I missed him often, usually while doing everyday tasks that reminded me of him. At the end of the day, I occasionally had moments of sadness. During the Unity Church remembrance service, I was happy for Bernie, yet I longed for him to be near me. The birthing of my first book, cause several emotions to surface. I felt excited yet heartbroken that I couldn't share it with Bernie—he wasn't there to see my success, which he always supported. It amazed me that I was able to maintain my emotional well-being and move on with my dignity intact so quickly.

Week Three

I continued to meet with clients as well as facilitate my group repatterning sessions. Betsy and I worked on marketing my newly published book and uploading my Facebook posts. Mid-week, I attended the Scottsdale Society of Women Writers monthly meeting, and completed my annual Worker's Compensation evaluation to continue treatment for my injured shoulder.

On Thursday, December 14, while doing my morning journaling, I heard Bernie loud and clear. I turned to a blank page in my journal and began writing what he said:

> *Oh, my beloved Victoria, I can only tell you how beautiful you are and how beautifully you took care of me till the very end and for all this I am eternally grateful. It is beautiful here. I know why my time was up on earth. I am meant to be an ambassador for change through you. We have a book to write. It's important. I know you have many extra tasks now that I am gone. I am sorry for being so stubborn and cheap. I want you to have all that life offers there. I want to take a moment to talk to you about my son. He is like me in a way—pushy, sometimes harsh and demanding. I make no excuse for his behavior, only that you soften your heart and send love. I understand your response. Your ability to step back and move forward is very humbling.*
>
> *Your idea to give my boys some money is a good one. Yes, I agree to give some of my ashes to be placed next to Oma and eventually Opa. Oma says hi as does your father, who wants to congratulate you on your book. I miss holding you Victoria and I know I am meant to be here. Call on Robert and Hans, they will help. OMG, one dumpster on my behalf. I am so grateful—one more to go. Dunny and Manny will help too. I will be around for a little while longer, and then I need to concentrate on my next mission. You'll know when it's time to dictate my book. I go but I stay. You are so loved and respected. Your Beloved Bernie.*

On Saturday, I took part in a meditation and sound healing event and the next day I went to the Unity Church service. I was a busy girl. As I returned to my very active life, I continued to feel Bernie's presence every day.

On Monday, Bernie's three sons and Robert came over for the reading of the will. He left it all to me—the house, its mortgage, its contents, and a few additional assets, with the promise that if there was any house money left when I died, I'd split it amongst his sons. They all knew there was no life insurance.

I found three $100 bills in Bernie's papers, just enough to give one to each of them—how fortunate. When I handed them the cash, each of them had a different reaction—his oldest thanked me, his middle son just grumbled about the amount, and his youngest told me to keep the money since I needed it and he didn't. I instantly welled up with tears, *"Your father would want you to have this, so please receive it from him."* The boys spent about two hours going through their father's things, taking a few mementos and some clothes that carried meaning for them.

After everyone left, I realized how stressful this experience was for me. Having the Higher Vibrations choir available that evening restored my spirit and filled my heart with hope and love.

This week was tougher than last week. Although, receiving a message from Bernie left me feeling warm and fuzzy inside, the reading of Bernie's will and his middle son's reaction to my $100 offer had been unsettling. Realizing that I wasn't the only person grieving, allowed me to express more compassion and love for everyone. Overall, three weeks after my beloved's death, I think I was doing rather well. I attributed this to all the delightful conversations we had and all the ways we loved each other.

Week Four

My first Christmas without Bernie was, understandably, not the same.

During the week, I did healing sessions with Paula and three other clients, as well as working with Betsy on my publishing website. I made time to get my hair done and have a massage to prepare for the holidays. Unity Church's Christmas services on Wednesday evening and Sunday morning were inspiring. Although it felt lonesome to be there without my beloved, both services strengthened my spiritual connection. I missed my Bernie!

Christmas Eve, I attended dinner at the home of Bernie's former wife. It was our tradition so Bernie could spend time with his boys. However, this year it felt uncomfortable. I didn't have much to say, especially after my hurtful experience with his middle son. It felt empty without my beloved. I missed my Bernie!

Christmas was on Monday. I spent the afternoon with my mom, we made lunch, took a walk through the park near her home, opened presents, and shared fond memories about Bernie—it was bittersweet. Then I went to my friend Linda's home for dinner. She made a wonderful meal and we shared heartfelt memories of by beloved. I missed my Bernie!

Week Five

I didn't see clients during the week between Christmas and New Year's to concentrate on finishing the marketing work on my book with Betsy. I also resumed my continuing education classes for my Repatterning Practitioner's Certification renewal.

Robert had promised Bernie to help me keep the house until I could decide what to do with it. I spent Thursday with Robert reflecting about good times with Bernie and planning to renovate the front bedroom. I wanted to turn it into a peaceful space for me to see clients, allowing me to save money by not paying rent for an office.

Over the next two days, I attended a session with Torina and visited friends. On New Year's Eve, I went to the Unity Church service, then home to relax and get ready for the formal dinner-dance at the Fatcat Ballroom. It was my first official dance event since Bernie's death. Sitting with my friend

Linda and her date, I felt like a third wheel. Luckily, there were plenty of men to dance with—it was fun to be out again.

Wow, what a year. Bernie and I did many things that made our last months, weeks, days, and hours, a time of deep understanding and enrichment of our relationship. We reminisced about all the fun, gratifying, and unique experiences we shared living together, traveling together, loving together.

As Bernie and I deepened our connection through healing our past, he saw what could be possible by mending his relationships with family and friends. Luckily, he had the time and opportunity to express his love, gratitude, and appreciation for what other people had contributed to his life before he died. Having cleaned the slate, our love kept expanding right up to the end. He encouraged me to love again, even bigger than the love we had—I couldn't imagine there was such a love, or that I would be ready any time soon.

Reviewing the intentions I created for this year, I realized I had met most of them just living my life, even with the overshadowing crisis of Bernie's illness and death. I published my first book, which became an Amazon bestseller. I definitely deepened my relationship with my beloved and enjoyed our travels this year—not knowing my travels with him would end so soon. Hands down I know I made an impact in Bernie's life and the lives of others, as my connections with people grew stronger. Given my circumstances, I did my best to live up to my standards for living and was pretty successful. I certainly expanded my capacity for compassion and generosity—especially by championing my beloved through his cancer and death. As for my emotional well-being, I was fortunate—Bernie and I had plenty of time and used it wisely to say our goodbyes.

I can speak about Bernie's goals only from my perspective. The two most important healings Bernie had were with his father and oldest son. In doing that, he became his greatest and highest self, and his relationships expanded to a deeper level. Bernie achieved his life's purpose of being a whole and complete expression of love as shown through his kind, loving, joyful, and adventurous spirit. Even though I made a start after his liberation, Bernie's desire that his house be a beautiful sanctuary did not happen—stay tuned to see what did happen.

Part 3

My Extraordinary Life

The Year of Adjustment

A new year begins—time to create my life without my Beloved Bernie. Where do I start?

In the beginning, I had many moments of missing Bernie—as I expected. Most days, I gracefully integrated into my new life, not having him by my side. I kept myself busy and made a lot happen because I had truly said goodbye, and I wasn't burdened with massive amounts of grief—although sometimes there he was in my mind and in my heart.

New Year's Day—time to evaluate the previous year's intentions and create possibilities for the coming year. It had only been five weeks since my beloved died making this process highly emotional. I was so used to having Bernie right there with me sharing our thoughts, ideas, and plans.

My major goals for 2018 in my transformational healing business were to continue serving my clients, promote my business through my website and social media, and move my office into my home. In my publishing business, my intentions included having my book reach #1 on Amazon; promoting my book through speaking engagements, book signings, and workshops; developing and facilitating new ways to support my readers; and publishing the first of my Fairy Realm books.

Beginning in the first week of January, I immersed myself in seeing four clients per week and facilitated my monthly in-person group sessions. Once again, I was glad to fully focus on clients when I was with them, instead of having Bernie's illness and death always at the back of my mind. It was so uplifting, especially when I followed up with them and they reported all the positive changes they were experiencing. It always left a warm feeling in my heart.

Most weeks, I worked two days with Betsy on reviewing my blog posts, updating my business website, and marketing my services on Facebook, Twitter, and LinkedIn. I kept myself busy, all the while knowing Bernie was watching over me.

Throughout the year, I spent considerable time coping with my mother's progressing dementia. Since she lived almost an hour away, I didn't always know what was happening day-to-day.

My book, *What Would Love Do Right Now?,* was already an Amazon bestseller at #12. When I was ready to inquire about book signings, speaking engagements, and other book promotion events, I knew the vendors would be more interested if the book was at #1. I hired Denise Cassino, an online book promoter, who had launched over 500 books to bestseller status on Amazon. She advised me that the best time for promotion was when my eBook was published.

Over the next few months, my presence on Social Media platforms was established to improve current book sales. We created the eBook launch plan and set it for May 18. It included designing twelve ads to be posted on launch day. I met weekly with Paula and Betsy to perfect the layout and design to be ready for the big day. It was demanding, yet exciting!

Besides working to get the eBook ready, I submitted my draft manuscript for my first fiction book, *Conversations with the Fairy Realm,* to be reviewed by Paula and Betsy. I hoped this book would be my next publication.

In mid-January, I had my first-ever vendor booth at the Scottsdale Library Independent Authors Book Sale. It was validating to engage with the many readers who were interested in my approach to living an extraordinary life. Yay—book sales!

That same week, I got a call from an investor friend of mine to see how I was doing without Bernie. During our conversation, he offered to do an unofficial appraisal of my home and make me a no-obligation offer. The offer he eventually presented was insultingly low, and I took a pass. Selling Bernie's home—which was now mine—was not even on my radar, but at least I had a bottom-line offer.

Bernie hadn't wanted any funeral celebration. He did ask me to take his family and some friends to dinner at the Hibachi Grill, right up the street from us. We often went to this all-you-can-eat buffet for family celebrations. I made plans for a group of us to go to there on Sunday, January 28 to celebrate Bernie's life.

Bernie's oldest and youngest sons, his younger brother and nephew from Germany, his former wife and her husband, along with our good friends Christopher and Robert, all showed up. I was pleased, as some of the group could not attend the *Celebrate Life with Bernie* event last October.

I brought a framed picture of Bernie and set it at the head of the table. It felt like he was joining us. I shared with the server why we were there, and she kindly offered her condolences and welcomed us back.

My intention for this gathering was to sincerely honor how Bernie had influenced the people who were there. I suggested everyone could share something they valued about their relationship with him. Bernie's youngest son spoke about how his father encouraged him to deal with his feelings in a positive way. His nephew mentioned how much he appreciated Bernie for always being so upbeat. Two people—that was it.

It became a gathering without a reason, and I felt like everyone was only there for a free dinner. I was so hurt and disappointed. I mustered up compassion for them, realizing they might not want to share their grief in an environment where they could be overheard and observed by strangers.

The following day, Bernie's relatives from Germany came over to the house for a visit. They wanted to know more about Bernie's last few weeks. I gladly shared with them what happened before, during, and after his death. They listened attentively and were both moved. Tears flowed and their heart's burst open as I spoke of the love Bernie and I shared. They were genuinely pleased that I was such a champion on Bernie's behalf.

When they returned to Germany, Bernie's father wanted to hear what I had shared with them. Bernie's nephew setup a phone call and translated our conversation. Bernie's father was deeply moved and thanked me for loving Bernie for so long and for being there for him in the last months of his life. I received his acknowledgment and kind words, which provided a deeper connection and healing between us.

Early in February, I took a day to acknowledge the support we had received from Bernie's surgeon and the Limb Center. I bought two thank you cards and bunches of flowers as tokens of my appreciation.

I knew Dr. Jacobsen saw patients at his office on Wednesdays, so I drove over to thank him and his staff for the wonderful care they provided. They were highly professional, kind, and compassionate when listening to Bernie's concerns, and always honored his choices.

As soon as I walked into his waiting room, my eyes welled up and I turned around and went outside to calm down. When I went back in and up to the nurses' station, the nurse who was most involved with Bernie's care recognized me and came running over to hug me. Then three other nurses, who also took care of him, came out to greet me. I told them Bernie had passed and a little of my story about being with Bernie at his last breath. They had tears in their eyes.

I waited until Dr. Jacobsen came out of the patient area. When he saw me, he stopped what he was doing to spend a few minutes with me. I acknowledged him for his warmth, his professionalism, and all the excellent care he provided Bernie, then handed him the flowers. He said that he was sorry for my loss and that it had been an honor to care for Bernie. He told me he felt the love I shared with Bernie and knew he would be missed.

Then, I went to The Limb Center to express my sincere gratitude to the staff. The owner, Dave, and the prosthetic assistant, David, greeted me. I was thrilled to acknowledge them for the way they went above and beyond the call of duty. Finding Bernie a prosthesis in the first place, and then all the extra work David did to get Bernie's new leg to fit—all without reimbursement. I handed the flowers and card to Dave. Several members of the staff expressed their gratitude for the opportunity they had to provide Bernie the chance to walk on both legs before he passed—restoring his dignity. They asked about my experience being present at Bernie's last breath. I didn't keep anything back. They listened sympathetically and were moved to tears.

They asked how I was doing and I let them know that although I had my moments, I was doing pretty well. I mentioned that the week after Bernie died I published my first book on Amazon. After I shared what it was about, Dave said, *"It sounds like your book is exactly what I need."* He was so excited he bought one right out of my trunk.

I could feel the positive impact my visit had on everyone. I was delighted. It was gratifying to be able to honor the medical and personal care bestowed upon Bernie.

Even though Bernie was no longer available to me physically, we remained connected spiritually, and he often communicated with me directly.

Three days after my first Valentine's Day without Bernie, I was having my morning coffee and heard a knock at my front door. When I opened it, to my surprise, there was a Happy Valentine's Day balloon and a bouquet of flowers that looked about a week old, sitting on my porch. I ran out to see who had dropped them off and there was no one to be found. Thanks Bernie! The flowers brought a smile to my face and reminded me that Bernie would buy flowers earlier in the week, so it would fit his budget, hold on to them for the big day, and then give them to me. Bless his heart! I took it as a sign he was around, still loving me.

February was packed with book promotions and supporting my readers. I spent the first two weeks developing a half-day workshop and a 12-week course—both titled, *Design Your Ideal Life from the Power of Love.*

As soon as I finished creating these projects, I facilitated my first 12-week course with eight women. We took a deep dive into using my *Inquiry to Resolution* process for healing incidents from the past. Each week the participants eagerly examined a different aspect of their lives. We covered relationships with family, friends, and co-workers; health; finances; and self expression. It was transformational, and they consistently reported how these healings made a difference for them. The interactions with these women and the progress they made during the course helped to fill the void in my heart.

The Feng Shui Festival, scheduled two days after my first course session, was a terrific opportunity to promote both my transformational healing practice and my bestselling book. As I was gathering what I needed for my booth, it suddenly dawned on me that I was so used to having Bernie there, I had not arranged for anyone to support me. I had to transport supplies and have someone available to interact with people when I was busy or away from the booth. I reached out to my friend Christina, who was available—what a life saver! She did an amazing job working with me to set everything up, as well as answering questions and processing sales—thank you, Christina!

The event organizer invited me to give a brief introduction about my book to a gathering of attendees. Although I was somewhat nervous to be speaking to an audience of people I didn't know, it was invigorating to inspire them to make positive changes in their lives. Book sales—Yay!

The following week I held my first half-day workshop at Reverend Tina's Unity Celebration Church. I introduced the concepts and transformational practices discussed in my book, inspiring the participants to buy a copy and use it on their own to heal their past and create a more promising future. More book sales—Yay!

Starting at the end of February, Paula and I spent two days sorting Bernie's clothes and personal belongings, which wasn't the easiest process. We tackled his dresser, under-bed storage, and closet, all of which were tightly packed with shirts, sweaters, suits, uniforms, casual clothes, belts, ties, socks, and shoes. I was so proud of myself for letting go of so much so quickly. There were only two shirts I couldn't imagine releasing—the Hawaiian shirt he wore when we got married that had such significant sentimental value, and his peach shirt that always made him look incredibly sexy.

The Monday after we were done sorting, Paula brought her friend Wayne over to help me figure out what to do with Bernie's clothes. He knew what kind of clothing would be useful to donate to Andre House, a ministry to the homeless and poor populations in the Phoenix area. The last place we cleared that day was the hall closet. We found several outdoor jackets and 25 pair of shoes—some of which were holding up the shelves. When we got to Bernie's favorite jacket, I burst into tears. The same thing happened when I came across his favorite pair of shoes. It was a tough day. Both Wayne and Paula just let me have my feelings, without judgment or trying to fix me. They were supportive, and I expressed my gratitude to both of them. We filled Wayne's van to the brim, and off they went. I kept a few designer suits and sweaters I hoped to sell, and packed up what was left and took it to the Salvation Army.

The next day, I had HAD IT—I was fed up and angry. I looked at Bernie's picture; pointed my finger right at him; raised my voice; and gave him a piece of my mind. *"Not only did you die on me, you left me with a ton of paperwork and all your s**t to release—what the F***! I am tired of going through your crap. It's taking me hours of my precious time to clean up your TRASH. What were you thinking? When were you ever going to get rid of things you no longer needed? You OWE ME—big time!"* Then suddenly, I burst into tears, held the picture close to my heart, and cried and cried. Expressing my anger helped me to feel my deep love for Bernie.

On Wednesday, I called my friend Roxane, who is an energy healer. She and I exchanged sessions during the ten years Bernie and I were together and she knew a lot about our relationship. I told her I felt like I had five jobs; my job running my healing business; my job promoting my book; my job helping my mom cope with how her life was changing; my job of releasing Bernie's belongings; and my job of settling Bernie's estate.

Roxane stated, *"You may want to consider that rather than thinking you have five jobs, you actually have five areas in your life that you are giving loving service to."* That comment changed my whole attitude and set me free to see my previous jobs as opportunities to show love. I began making lists of everything I was up to, scheduling time to take care of these five areas, and adding fun social activities, so my life was more balanced and didn't feel like work—work—work! Thank you, Roxane!

At the beginning of March, it was time to start working on clearing the apartment. Paula and I took a day to go through the laundry room and the bathroom. We bagged up what we thought someone else might use and took it all to Goodwill—and so it began. Robert and Paula spent a few days working on the living room. We were surprised to find a couch at the bottom of the pile of empty boxes. Robert told me that a few years before I moved in, he mentioned to Bernie, *"When you pass, some poor sucker will have to clean this mess."* Little did he know that *"that poor sucker"* would end up being him! While they worked on the apartment, I continued clearing Bernie's bedroom and bathroom. I wasn't ready yet to tackle the huge piles of Bernie's treasures in the apartment on my own—I knew I would get to it sooner or later.

Since I wasn't ready to sell the house, Robert and I discussed what it would take to turn the front bedroom into a home office, which would save me $450 a month in office rent. For the sake of convenience and saving time, Robert stayed with me during the 3-month renovation. We had been friends for ten years and enjoyed each other's company, shared good food, and many rich conversations—we both missed Bernie.

Robert worked on the room a little each day. It took a couple of weeks just to clear the space—it was floor to ceiling junk, including a bunk bed we didn't know was lurking there. At the end of the month, Robert started the work creating my new office. He eliminated the scorpion and ant infestations in the ceiling—he killed over 100 scorpions and didn't get stung once. He then repaired the ceiling and the roof, painted the entire room, and laid new carpet. He also added crown molding and new baseboards, installed a new window, put up a ceiling light, and made contractor quality shelves to store my office supplies and everything I needed to serve my clients. Then I, yes I, made drapes for the closet. I hadn't used my sewing machine in years, I don't know what came over me. Robert helped to make sure the pattern for both panels matched perfectly—they were stunning!

In his spare time, Robert tackled areas of the backyard and a few more things inside. He emptied three of the sheds and started cleaning out the semi-trailer, where he found two king size mattresses and box springs. The tools went to his brother, and one of Bernie's sons selected some things to repurpose himself. What was left went out for bulk trash collection. Next, he hung a new front door, painted my security door, changed all the switch plates in my entire house, and chopped two tons of wood for my fireplace. I was extremely appreciative for all of Robert's support. My hero!

On March 17, I was journaling in the morning and, out of the blue, Bernie came in loud and clear—I wrote what I heard.

> *Oh, my beloved wife, it is so beautiful here—so serene, so captivating. I have finished my life review and am choosing my next assignment—my journey. I have been asked to be an ambassador for truth. One of the ways to accomplish this is through you taking my dictation and writing a book to help ease people's fear of dying. There are so many on earth who are holding on because of fear. This book will help with this for many.*
>
> *On a more personal note, I love you dearly, as earthly love goes. I can still say that you made me feel love and loved, for which I am eternally grateful. I have been informed of your progress and I commend you for who you are during this time of transition. It's okay to release the house if that's what you choose. Thank you for loving my children. I miss them too. It is so expansive here. Feel my arms around you. I miss the touch as well. Not that you need my permission for anything, however, I want you to know it's okay to make love with someone else. I'm working on sending you someone magnificent, just like you are visualizing. I'm glad my son took the couch. I am proud of him. Please tell him so.*
>
> *Until we talk again, know you are loved—so loved, so loved.*

This confirmed my idea of writing a book about my life with Bernie and his liberation. To capture my experience, I often wrote notes about what was happening, how I was responding, and how I was processing my loss. Now I was also eager to include his wisdom in the book. I realized I was not a weeping widow—what a perfect title! I just needed to keep writing as the spirit moved me.

On another note, hearing it was okay to release the house if I chose was music to my ears. I also allowed myself to take in his permission to love again when I was ready, which I didn't think would be anytime soon. It was exhilarating to know his love for me was still present. I love you too, Bernie!

I attended a Torina channeling event on the last Friday of the month, where Brenda relayed Bernie's message to me.

> *Thank you for loving me the way you have, never giving up on me and yes, you are the love of my life. Thank you for everything, for accepting my choice. Keep loving with your huge heart!*

These unexpected messages from Bernie contained acknowledgment and gratitude for the many ways I loved him. I let his message permeate the core of my being in a grand and glorious manner.

Only three months after my beloved's death, I realized I was remarkably present and fully engaged in moving on. I was not disoriented, devastated, or paralyzed, as one might expect for such a recent and significant loss. Yes, I had moments of sadness. Yes, I had moments of frustration. Yes, I had moments of missing Bernie.

My friend Donna from Santa Fe, came to visit for four days in April—we went dancing, shopping, eating, and hung out with some of my friends. We had a blast, and I felt completely supported!

After she left, I was surprised to have a short romance come my way. While Robert was working on my office, we sensed a developing fondness between us. We started cuddling and kissing occasionally—it seemed a little too soon, and OMG, with Bernie's best friend? At first, it felt like I was betraying Bernie, but then I remembered he told me to not wait around and to love again. My romance with Robert would have to wait.

My journey to honor my beloved husband's wishes to have his ashes released in the ocean near Kauai began on April 14. Besides fulfilling Bernie's wish, I had two personal intentions related to my bestselling book. One was to sell at least two copies of the book. The other was to visit The Talk Story bookstore in Hanapepe, introduce myself to the owner, request he carry my book, and schedule a book signing for August.

When the plane touched down on Kauai at 3:30 in the afternoon, it was pouring down rain. I had rented a car through a company that Bernie and I had used in the past— they always picked us up at the airport and took us to their off-site location. This time, in place of a ride, I received a text letting me know their shuttle was unavoidably unavailable and telling me to take a taxi to their lot at my own expense.

I was surprised not to get an—Aloha, welcome to Kauai— from my taxi driver. Instead, I was driven by a surly Hawaiian who didn't say a word, dropped me off in the pouring rain, and promptly left after I paid the fare.

When I reached the car rental lot, the office was closed, there was no attendant on duty, and no cover from the rain—I was on my own. I immediately texted the company—"I can't find the car that you assigned to me." They texted back—"Oh, by the way, we have a different rental car for you. It's in space C4." I finally found the filthy, little Rent-a-Wreck that had a note on the dash—NO TRUNK ACCESS—Yikes!

This created a brand new dilemma. Where am I going to put my luggage? The car was a small 2-door coupe and only the passenger's side seat would collapse forward to access the back seat. This tiny car presented a major challenge. I had to wrestle my large 50lb suitcase into the back by myself. All the while, I was standing in a torrential downpour, becoming increasingly frustrated. Where's my Bernie when I need him? Oh yeah, he's in the suitcase.

Before I could leave the lot, I had to read and sign the rental agreement. To handle that out of the rain, I got in the car. When I tried to get out to put the contract and the money in the drop box, the automatic door lock on the driver's side was stuck, so I couldn't open the door. Did I mention it was an itty-bitty car? I'm a petite woman, nonetheless, I was stuck. Eventually, I wiggled out from behind the steering wheel, crawled over the console, and exited the vehicle through the passenger door. Then, I scurried as quickly as I could to the drop box, shoved everything in, and ran back to the car. Fortunately, I could unlock the driver's door with the key to get back in. There I sat—alone, soaking wet, frustrated, on the verge of tears, and missing my husband, who usually handled issues such as these. Intending to ease my frustration by listening to some Hawaiian music and getting into the Aloha spirit, I turned on the radio. Damn, it didn't work either.

I knew I had two choices—I could choose to be a victim of my circumstances or acknowledge myself for my perseverance and resourcefulness. Taking a few deep breaths, I declared out loud, "I am in Kauai, the Garden Island of the Universe. What problems could there possibly be?" Setting the GPS for the nearest Costco, away I went in the pouring rain—on what was becoming my grand adventure in paradise.

Thankfully, by the time I left Costco with enough food for the week, it had stopped raining. I was strategically putting the groceries in the car on the passenger's seat and floor, knowing I would have to crawl over them to get out at my destination.

As I finished arranging the food, a gorgeous Hawaiian man, who was parked next to me, locked eyes with mine—it was heavenly!

He asked, "Wow, where did you come from and where are you going?"

I responded, "Ha'ena."

"You won't get there. The roads are closed. They'll put you up in a shelter, so you might as well come home with me. I'll show you a very good time."

Oh my! My heart skipped a beat and with no hesitation I said, "I don't doubt that for a moment!"

I drove off with my good judgment intact, not knowing if he was giving me a line or being truthful—my ego was pumped, he was young enough to be my son.

With my mind now lost in lust, and with raindrops again dancing on my windshield, I continued alone on my adventure to reach my vacation accommodations. After traveling north for about an hour, it became obvious that he was right—my GPS showed ROADS CLOSED DUE TO FLOODING. OMG, what an adventure, what else could possibly happen? Taking a deep breath, I pulled into the nearest gas station to confirm that the roads were indeed closed—they were. I was now stranded on a lonely stretch of highway, in the rain, in the dark, with plenty of food, and nowhere to stay. Where I was originally going, disaster was striking. The storm hit right before I arrived, and the north part of the island was experiencing the aftermath. Helicopters were flying in food for people unable to get out of the area or back to their homes.

Suddenly Bernie's friend Gene, who lived on the island, popped into my head, so I gave him a call. He knew I was coming to the island, and we had plans to meet up, but I had no idea where his house was. My luck turned around; he was home and lived only ten minutes from where I was. He graciously said, "Come on over, I'll find you somewhere to stay in my house." What a miracle!

There were other castaways staying at Gene's place who couldn't get to work, so all of us had a wonderful week! We had long enriching conversations and delectable community dinners. There was even a ballroom dance instructor there, so we danced the night away a few times—how cool is that? What were the odds that a random storm would cause the roads to be impassable, making it impossible to get to my original destination? Destiny!

Gene's property was between Anahola and Kilauea at an elevation above the flooding. I showed my book to everyone at Gene's place and gave them a couple of colorful wristbands that read, What Would Love Do Right Now? They were all excited and grateful that they had extra wristbands to share with some of their friends. Wearing the wristband would be a reminder to ask this question throughout the day and follow their heart's response. My mission to make the question, What Would Love Do Right Now?, a household trend and help people live more heart-centered lives, was working! I was absolutely thrilled to give a woman at Gene's place two extra books and wristbands that she planned to sell in the gift shop where she worked on the island. Speaking of gifts, Gene saw the value of my book right away and bought one as a wedding present for his son and new daughter-in-law. I was walking on air!

When I awoke on Tuesday, I saw that the sun was coming out from its long hiatus. I knew it was the day to release Bernie's ashes to the sea. I put on my bathing suit and a beach wrap, gathered what I planned to read during the ceremony, plus a photo of Bernie, his ashes, a blanket, water, as well as a few essential oils.

Gene drove me to Moloaa Beach, which was five minutes down the road, and waited for me in the car. I let him know I might be an hour, and I didn't want ANY pressure to leave at any specific time. He said, "Okay, not a problem. I've wanted to catch up on my reading, so this is perfect."

It was magnificent to be greeted by the sea and the sunshine, which was a special treat that day. I walked down the path from the parking lot, passing a few couples basking in the sun. They reminded me of the ten years of walking and picnicking with Bernie on all the breathtaking beaches we had visited from the Caribbean to the coasts of Mexico, Florida, California, and Hawaii. I was also reminded of Lake Zell in Austria, as well as the many lakes we enjoyed in Wisconsin, Wyoming, and at home in Arizona. The memories flooded my body.

I saw in the distance the perfect spot where I wanted to have Bernie's release ceremony. It was difficult to walk in my tennis shoes as the sand was heavy and wet from the several days of torrential rains and flooding. I persisted, and was glad that I hadn't worn my sandals. Both bags I was carrying, one with the supplies and the other with the urn of Bernie's ashes, were getting heavier and heavier by the minute. When I arrived at the spot, I laid the blanket down and stayed there for about ten minutes, soaking up the sun on my face and body.

The time came—Bernie picked it, I am sure. I set out everything I brought and announced the beginning of the ceremony. I put Bernie's picture right in front of me, and a photo of Bruno Groening, one of Bernie's spiritual teachers, to the left. My eyes welled up with sadness and joy at the same time, which I was getting really good at. I began by spraying rose oil in the area around me, smelling the essence of the love we shared. I then recited aloud poetry I had chosen, along with some of the letters, cards, and poems I had received from Bernie over the years.

Our Friendship©

We have formed
a friendship
that has become
invaluable to me
We discuss our goals
and plan our future
We express our fears
and talk about our dreams
We can be very serious
or we can just have fun
We understand each other's lives
and try to encourage each other
in all that we do
We have formed
a friendship
that makes our lives
so much
nicer

~ Susan Polis Schutz

Letter to me from Bernie

I'm sorry that I didn't recognize the importance of your heart, which needed some recognition from me. I was not in a good moment at the time when you asked last year for a contribution to the wedding ring you found, bought, and loved.

I'd like to make it up to you with a small token and contribution to your beautiful ring, which means so much to you, so you always know that I am here to support you and make up for my shortcomings.

May this ring be a sign of our shared love together, even if sometimes I am blocked through whatever circumstance to recognize this.

Please forgive me for this weak moment in my life and we both know that love will supersede everything from this moment on.

From the bottom of my heart, I'd like to make a contribution so that we can be 100% again in our fantastic relationship. No matter what, our love will supersede anything and everything in the physical realm.

I love you unconditionally from the bottom of my heart. I gave you everything I own so you can experience my love.

~ Bernie

For the Love of My Life

Whatever life brings
as we go through the years
it's wonderful knowing
you're there,
sharing your faith
and your beautiful heart
in the partnership
you and I share.
So, my love, I just wanted
to tell you today
that I'm grateful for all
that you do,
and I hope, in return,
I have proven to be
a loving companion
to you.

~ Bernie

My Friend©

My friend,
we have come such a long way
in the time that we've
known each other.

We've given each other
Encouragement
and have accomplished things
that we never thought
we could do.

I have become a better person
since knowing you.

You have given me many things
which I will treasure for a lifetime,
and the most important thing of all
is the gift of your friendship.

~ Laura Lee Leyman

Special©

"Special" is a word
that is used to describe
something one-of-a-kind
like a hug
or a sunset
or a person who spreads love
with a smile or kind gesture.

"Special" describes people
who act from the heart
and keep in mind the hearts of others.

"Special" applies to something
that is admired and precious
and which can never be replaced.

"Special" is the word that best
describes you.

~ Teri Fernandez

I Love You

I Love You
not only for who You are, but for who I am
when I am with You.

I Love You
not only for what You have made of yourself
but for what You are making of me.

I Love You
for ignoring the possibilities of the fool in me
and for laying firm hold of the possibilities for good.

I Love You
for closing your eyes to the discords
and for opening the music in me by your tender listening.

I Love You
for helping me to make of my life, a temple
and out of the words of every day, a song.

I Love You
because you have done more
than any creed to make me happy.
You have done it without a word,
without a touch, without a song.
You have done it just by being yourself
after all, this is what Love means.

I Love You

~ Bernie

With Love on Your Birthday©

You're someone
who brings
happiness
to everyone you know,

The world's
a better place
somehow
wherever
you may go...

You're like a ray
of sunshine
that gives life
a warmer touch –
And that's the special reason
why you're loved
so very much.

And especially from me.

~ Unknown

My One and Only©

There's no one in the world
who's closer to me than you,
yet just when I think
I couldn't love you more,
there's always something new to discover
that makes our love more precious.

With every day, with every year,
you're dearer to me than ever before.

With Love from Your Forever Valentine

~ Unknown

Happy Anniversary to My Wife©

Thank you
for brightening
my heart, my life –
my world.

You're a very
special woman
and I'm so glad
I married you.

It is our Love which will
create our heaven/beach.
Thank you for being in my life.

~ Unknown

If I Could Reach Up©

If I could reach up
and hold a star
for each time
you've made me smile,
an entire evening's sky
would be in
the palm of my hand.

~ Rowland R. Hoskins, Jr.

Just as I was finishing the reading, I remembered the message I received from Bernie letting me know he still loved me. I spent about fifteen minutes releasing his ashes to the sea. He loved the sea, and the sea loved him. I could feel Bernie's presence with me, so grateful that I was releasing the body he lived in for 62 years. It was windy, and twice the ashes got all over me—his last way of hugging me, I'm sure. Afterward, I took time to reflect on our amazing life together, closing the chapter and moving on like he would want me to—I felt so free!

I packed up and went back to where Gene was waiting. He respectfully allowed for the silence I needed on the drive to his place. I know Bernie sent Gene my way during this sacred time. We all gathered again in the main house for dinner and evening festivities—great food, music, dancing, cards, games, and authentic conversations.

On Friday evening, the last day of my trip, I met Connie and Arnie at their Hanapepe Market and Art Night jewelry booth. Bernie and I became friends with them when we visited Kauai three years earlier. Connie was so excited for me that she bought a book. Two books sold—intention fulfilled! Later that night, I went to The Talk Story Book Store and exchanged contact information with the owner. Although he declined to add my book to his shelves right now, we discussed the possibility of a book signing and that I should contact him when I was ready—intention in the works.

My plan this trip had been to be on my own, relax, and honor Bernie's memory. It turned out to be so much more— turning circumstances I could have allowed to devastate me into an unexpected adventure of friendship, camaraderie, joy, love, and completion.

Back home from Kauai, I longed to feel settled in my environment, yet every time I looked around the house, Bernie's things were everywhere. A part of me felt comfortable because seeing his belongings was familiar and made me feel connected to him. Another part of me wanted a clutter-free sanctuary I could call my own. I knew somehow, someday, this would happen.

My Scottsdale Society of Women Writers monthly meeting was held three days after I returned from spreading Bernie's ashes. The speaker that month suggested we take a moment to write something spontaneous about travel—how perfect! I wrote this and mustered up the courage to share it:

> *The spirit of aloha permeates the moist air*
> *as it soaks into my dry Arizona skin.*
> *The people are interested in who I am*
> *and what I am all about.*
> *The green blanket of lush foliage wraps me*
> *with warmth and love, and feeds my soul.*

By the end of April, Robert had finished the renovations on my beautiful new home office, just in the nick of time. I had received a notice that my office rent was going up by $40 in May. Robert and another friend helped me move out of my old office into my new office. The move went smoothly—one trip and done. Yippee! I spent the rest of the day unpacking, sorting, and organizing, and began seeing clients the very next day—You Go Girl! It felt good to have my office in my home, which saved a lot of travel time and money. I was happy. Thanks Robert! You're the best!

After the office move was complete, Robert told me he realized, while I was in Kauai, that he wasn't ready to be in a relationship. I was glad he told me since I wasn't ready either even though it was nice to be held and cared for again. He said he needed to retreat inward to pursue his own spiritual path and would not be in communication with me for a while. I honored his wishes, and we had minimal contact for over two years—I missed him and our heartfelt conversations about life.

Now that my office was in place, I figured I better get started clearing out Bernie's treasures. If you're wondering why I just didn't have it all hauled away—I couldn't. Bernie said he wanted me to sell things for as much money as I could get. He also let me know, the week before he passed, that money was hidden in the house, although he didn't tell me where. At first, I felt betrayed because he had money stashed away that we could have used. Then I realized that if we were really in a jam financially, some money would be available. This also meant I had to look through every box, every shelf, and every folder—luckily, I found some cash in the file cabinets!

At the beginning of May, Paula and I packed up hundreds of VHS tapes, CDs, and books that were stacked up along the wall leading to the laundry room—one more clearing done. Yay! She and her friend Dorothy cleared more of my space by taking two huge televisions, all the stereo equipment, and six boxes of the tapes to a local school. I could then give away the giant entertainment center I no longer had a use for. More progress releasing treasures!

Getting rid of the vehicles Bernie left came next. I sold the Jeep to my neighbor. I had the junkyard tow away the Hyundai—they gave me $200. When Bernie's friend Dunny was ready to return to Belize, I gave him the speedboat, two jet skis, one of the hitch-trailers, and the green car to take back with him—he was overjoyed, and so was I. The rest of the year, I continued to honor Bernie's request to sell or donate items of value from the house when I could—often with the help of my friends.

May 18, eBook Launch Day! Hip-Hip-Hooray! I lowered the price on Amazon to $.99 for 24 hours, posted the ads Denise and I had created on Facebook and LinkedIn, and called my friends to let them know the eBook was available! Denise's Twitter posts went out every hour, and we were counting on some of her 20,000 followers to buy my eBook. It worked! In less than 12 hours, *What Would Love Do Right Now?* shot to the top of the list—I was an Amazon #1 Bestselling Author! I was ecstatic! I ran outside and jumped up and down like I just won the lottery. Then I called Denise, Betsy, and Paula to tell them the good news and to thank them from the bottom of my heart for all their assistance and collaboration. My adrenaline rush stayed with me all day.

The next day I gave an overview of my book and the *Inquiry to Resolution* process to a small meditation group hosted by my friend Janice. The participants were eager to hear about the benefits of the book and five people bought a copy right then and there. Yay! I didn't know how inspiring and thrilling this would be. I was on a roll, so a few days later, I gave myself a 3-day book retreat at home. The progress I made toward revising my second fiction book, *Adventures with the Fairy Realm,* was remarkably satisfying.

On Mother's Day, I drove out to see my mom, brought lunch, and gave her a beautiful card that moved her to tears. She once again reminded me not to worry about her because she was doing fine. I kindly asked to look at her mail, so I could keep up with things and she blew a gasket! *"Get out of my business! I'm doing just fine! I am handling things JUST FINE!"* I was so upset with her response that I left earlier than I had planned.

On Father's Day, I went to visit my mom again. It was good to see her. We went through the family photo album, which was exceptionally good for her brain. She remembered most of the people in the pictures. The day was delightful and I left hopeful this time.

Over the next several months, I discovered mom was not showing up for her doctor's appointments nor taking her medication regularly. She also started neglecting her house and her cats—all while fighting me tooth and nail to keep her independence and stay in her home. Keeping in mind what her social worker had said about letting her fail so she could get the help she needed, I realized how tough this was going to be—I did my best.

In June, I attended two group spiritual retreats with Dawn Katar, one early in the month and the other at the end. The time spent away from day-to-day concerns and distractions helped me center my energy in my heart, clarify my priorities, and deepen my connection with God. It was impactful and divine.

In between these retreats in Phoenix, I escaped the 110° heat by going up north where it was 20° cooler! I spent three days at the cabin in Breezy Pines by myself, enjoying the weather and long walks in the forest. It was the first time I went up there without my beloved. I recalled all the good times we had there and held the memories deep in my heart.

On June 23, I facilitated another workshop at Unity of Phoenix. Twelve people attended and ten of them were moved to buy books. Book sales—Yay! It felt good knowing that my efforts were going to make a positive difference in their lives.

In mid-July, three days before my first birthday without Bernie, I again heard a message from him.

> *My sweet Victoria, there are no words to express my gratitude and honor to have been loved by you. I am so proud of you. As your birthday approaches, know I am with you. Be sure to update your will so it includes all those who have so generously supported you. As you know, one never knows the time, unless you do.*
>
> *I feel so free. My lessons are even more intense here. Your father is so proud of you and wishes to tell you he loves you and to thank you for spending such quality time with him over the years. Gotta go. Know you are loved.*

Hearing this message warmed my heart and reassured me not only of Bernie's love, but of my father's as well. Not that I needed it, but it was really gratifying to hear.

On my birthday, I visited my mom and thanked her, like I do every year, for birthing me and taking care of me growing up. She knew it was my birthday and had a gift for me. I was pleasantly surprised that she had remembered. We shared lunch and then off I went to spend time with my friends that evening dancing the night away!

To reward myself for all of my work and book sales, I took two book retreats at the cabin in August. The first for two days early in the month and the second for five days at the end. It was fabulous to get away from the heat and sequester myself while focusing on completing the manuscript to hand over my second fiction book to Paula, my meticulous editor. What an incredible feeling of accomplishment!

Seven months after Bernie died, and a few months since Robert left, I felt it was time to get back into the dating scene. On a recommendation from a girlfriend I bought, *Getting Naked Again,* by Judith Sills, PhD, and spent the next weekend reading it. Basically, the author wrote that there were no rules. The book emphasized the benefits of getting out there and involving myself in the activities that were of interest and importance to me that I wanted to share with someone special. Then when someone asked me out, the idea was to just say yes and start dating. So, I embarked on discovering what type of man would be a good fit for me despite the author's warning that a few heartbreaks may occur along the way. Eventually a wonderful partner would show up—which is exactly what happened.

Since dancing is one of my primary social activities, this is where I met most of the men I dated. I arranged my schedule to ensure I went to the AZ Classic Dance Weekend on the first Saturday in August—I didn't want to miss the professional competitions and dinner show that evening.

I arrived ready to dance. Vince was there. He was someone I danced with at the Fatcat Ballroom many times. As soon as he saw me, he offered to buy me a glass of wine. I accepted his kind offer. We danced several times during the evening. He told me he knew I was there to dance, and he didn't want to monopolize my time, so he sat at another table. I thought that was rather considerate. After the next week's dance lesson at Fatcats, Vince and I went out for a drink and had fun getting to know each other better.

We started dating twice a week. He was originally from eastern Europe and had a cultural view that was different from mine. His accent required me to listen closely when he was speaking. I assumed it was the same for him. Right off the bat, I told him that as there were already lots of differences between men and women and we had the added challenge of cultural compatibility, making it imperative to communicate clearly and discuss what we didn't understand to avoid disagreements. One area I thought we might struggle with was creating time to be together since he own a business and I owned two businesses. Thankfully, he understood my limited availability.

The morning of August 29—Bernie's first birthday since his liberation—I received another message from him. He came through loud and clear.

> *Oh, my beloved Victoria, my time here has not been easy. I got a chance to see how my thoughts, words, and actions were hurtful and harmful. I got to see from others' perspective how I added insult to injury.*
>
> *As for my time with you, my sweet Victoria, I am so sorry for the times I cut you off in conversation. I am sorry for the times I spent on the computer rather than spending time with you when you came home from work. I realize that you spending so much time away in all your activities was partly because I wasn't available for you—yet it was the very thing I wanted most from you. I am especially sorry for my laziness and how it impacted our living space. It's hard to believe you stuck around as long as you did. I had the love I was longing for in you, yet I couldn't see it, so I had to have so many things*

around everywhere to feel abundant. I realize now how hard that was for you and even through all this, you loved me—you loved me BIG.

All this is in the record book, so when your time on earth is finished, it will be available for your review. I have another month of learning before I can be present for the download of your book. Stay tuned.

In the meantime, I am grateful for your continued love. I am grateful that Robert continues to step up and that your new boyfriend is there now to help you make wise choices and shower you with things and experiences I chose not to provide. I miss you at my side, yet I know you are in my heart. I'll stay for about another ten minutes in your time. Please stop writing and feel me and my love for you during these ten minutes. I will go then.

I love you, Victoria. You were the best thing that ever happened to me.

What a message! Amends from the other side—it doesn't get much better than that. It was tremendously valuable receiving his acknowledgment for the things I tolerated and accepted. I also understood that in order for him to feel abundant, he needed to surround himself with soooo much stuff. This explained a lot. I allowed Bernie's love for me to fill my heart in a big way.

When I visited my mom in August, I noticed she was repeating both questions I had already answered and things she had told me earlier. I started getting a little more worried about what was going to happen, and who was going to help me now that Bernie was gone. I just kept hanging in there.

On my first visit in September, my mom's house reeked of cats and was an absolute mess, which was totally out of character for her. Normally, she took exceptionally good care of her home and her pets, making sure her house was clean, and the cats' litter box was emptied every day. When I looked around, it was clear three or four days of dirty dishes were piled in the sink and the litter box hadn't been cleaned for a week—disgusting! Also, I could tell my mom was confused about when and how much she was feeding the cats—or not. She appeared not to be aware of the stench or the mess and was appalled to realize she wasn't looking after her well-loved pets. I spent a couple of hours vacuuming, dusting, scouring the kitchen, and cleaning up after the cats.

Mom's behavior and the condition of her home seriously concerned me, so I went back the following week—the litter box was a mess and the sink was full again! I talked to my mom's friend and neighbor, Carmen, and arranged with her to check in on my mother daily and make sure the cats were fed and the litter box was cleaned. Knowing she would call me if something unusual happened, provided me with a respite from daily worry. Of course, I paid her for her time, which was truly priceless. Seeing my mom begin to fail in this way left me feeling helpless and heartbroken.

On October 8, I went with my mom to see her doctor. Her blood pressure was 200/98. The doctor told me to take her to the Emergency Room at once, which I did. At the ER, they gave her an immediate dose of blood pressure medication and a saline IV for dehydration. Even though she insisted she took her pills as directed, clearly that was not the case—I didn't know for how long or how often she had been lax in taking them. When we got back to her house, I asked Carmen to add giving my mother her medication to the list of things she was already doing to support her. I tried to have Carmen hold the medication at her place and bring it over each day—my mom absolutely refused to cooperate, and maintained she was doing everything she was supposed to do! Letting her fail was now downright frightening.

From the get-go, Vince was exceptionally generous, something I was not used to. He took me shopping and bought me several cool summer outfits. I was moved to tears—no man had ever done that for me. When he started buying towels and sheets that I didn't need, it seemed odd—hmmm PINK FLAG.

In mid-September, Vince and I spent a playful weekend in Rocky Point, Mexico. On the drive home, we had a disagreement related to the timeshare presentation we attended—he didn't want to talk about it, so we drove back to Phoenix in silence. RED FLAG!

During the week following the trip to Mexico, I casually mentioned to Vince that I wanted the huge lantana bush in my front yard trimmed. He made it absolutely clear that he thought I should remove it altogether, which I told him I did not want done. He generously hired a landscaper in my neighborhood to do the work. When I came home that evening, the lantana I loved was GONE—I was shocked. When I called Vince to let him know how upset I was that he had disrespected me, he was clueless about why I would be so offended. He offered to buy a replacement plant. I told him that was not the point—the point was that he deliberately did what I clearly had asked him not to do. RED FLAG #2!!

I began noticing how often Vince questioned me about where I went, what I was doing, who I was with—it was disconcerting. I'm a free spirit and I love being social with all sorts of people doing things I love whenever I want. It became clear that Vince expected me to be someone other than who I was. RED FLAG #3!!! At one point, he started asking me to change my already healthy personal hygiene habits—he was obsessed with me taking showers— GIGANTIC RED FLAG!!!!!

After dating Vince for a couple months, I realized we had little to talk about. Aside from dancing, he and I had no common interests, especially spiritually, which was very important to me.

The last straw for me with Vince came a few weeks later. He had me over to his home for a meal. He served food he knew I was avoiding, due to a health condition, and then was angry that I didn't eat every single thing that was offered. Afterward, as he was washing the dishes, I took a clean towel out of the drawer and started drying, he went off the deep end—talk about a control freak.

Finally clear that this would never work for me, I told Vince I wasn't interested in seeing him anymore and left. Although I had hoped to remain friends, it didn't happen that way. When I saw him at dance lessons, it was awkward partnering with him during the rotation—over time, it got better.

Heartbreak number one. I discovered I did not want someone controlling me—good thing to learn. What a wild start to my search for a new romantic partner. I didn't venture out into the dating world again for a few months.

On October 20, I received the first of five daily messages from Bernie. He wanted to make sure his messages got in this book.

Message on Day 1

My sweet, sweet, Victoria. I miss you so much. I miss your arms around me and my arms around you. Your love made my transition so much easier—especially at the end, which is actually the beginning. Leaving the physical body was easy; going through the veils was not so easy. The veils are layers of density—consciousness density. They are like energy veils, levels of density. There were five in my case. The first one was the hardest because I didn't want to leave just yet. I wanted to hang around for a while to make sure you were okay. Also, that the boys were okay.

The moments right after my last earthly breath were the most spectacular. It felt so free to be liberated from my physical body. My spirit was enormous—it filled the room, as you remember so vividly. It felt like I could create and manifest

*anything. In fact, when I thought of someone, they were there.
I kept waiting for The Creator and realized there was no
Creator—I was my own Creator.*

*What helped me move to the next energy veil was the
song you and the Higher Vibrations choir sang for me called,
Fly Away Home. That sent me through the next energy level,
similar to a wave of energy. Since there is no time and no space
really, only moments of now and now and now, the next layer
was more magnanimous.*

*The first person I saw was my mother, Maria, who held out
her hand for me. The second was Bruno Groening, who also
reached out his hand. These were not literal hands. Everything
was more energetic. Yet I knew somehow, they were assisting
me to the next energy density that I needed to enter to process
and merge through. This particular layer or density was the
toughest for me because it seemed like there were mirrors all
over. I couldn't move without looking at my spirit and my
humanity. I stayed at this level for what seemed to be days,
which are very hard to measure in no time. It felt like five earth
days.*

*Here I sat with my spiritual committee—other beings
of light whose job it was to help me look at my life through
both the eyes of spirit and the contract I had agreed to before
incarnating. It was not pretty, although between the hardships,
were acknowledgments of the difference I made. It's amazing
the amount of people I hurt along the way—some knowingly
and some unknowingly—through my stubbornness and lack
of empathy and compassion for others.*

*The third layer was wrought with releasing the guilt from
the pain and suffering I caused others, as well as the pain and
suffering others caused me. I was told my friend Gerhart had*

already reincarnated, so I didn't get to see him. It's not really seeing, it's more of a feeling, feeling the energy.

You think it's crowded on earth—you should see it here—souls everywhere. There are so many lost souls—energy beings with no interest in getting guidance. My project is to teach these souls about other options so they could choose to look into their mirrors and their shortcomings; the harm they created; and also release the seeming harm done to them by others. The concept we learned about is accurate. We pick our lessons for each incarnation, and we pick the players we need who are willing and agree to play the role. Just like you agreed to play the role of lover and friend with me for the time we had.

The mirror work was very random. I thought it would be more in linear time from conception to 62—not for me. It was more organized in feelings. I got to look at all the incidents where I felt betrayed and then how my words and actions, or lack of words and actions caused others to feel betrayed. I am actually still at this level. It is grueling, informative, and eye opening.

My spiritual committee consists of Bruno Groening, St. Germain, and Mother Mary. We go back to the beginning of time and have worked together many times for each other's evolution. One thing I learned was that Avatars are in their own process of becoming, of growing, of healing, of expansion. It is time for me to go now. More tomorrow—I love you, Victoria. All is well. We are one.

Message on Day 2

Oh, my sweet Victoria. Tender is your energy and your heart. Thank you for loving me all those years and all the years to come. I want to share a new project I'll be starting when our transmissions are complete. I am doing the prep work now. There is so much destruction of mother earth and I am now the ambassador of her reconstruction. I will be assisting key people in the areas of the world that have undergone massive destruction.

I'll be starting in the Hawaiian Islands, first Kauai, then Kona. There is some underground grid repair that is needed. I will be overseeing this project and even going into the trenches myself if need be. Let Carol in Kauai know of these efforts, and Lynette in Kona. Ask them to meditate on seeing the energy grid repaired. This will help our efforts. I will be heading up a team of twelve. Each area will take two weeks in your earth time to complete. We will begin on your date Friday, October 27. We will take one earth day off in between and then go to Kona. Be sure to put this in your book so others know it was completed. You can also help by visualizing the grid repaired during the time it is happening. Know you are loved beyond measure. Go now, enjoy your hike. I love you, Victoria.

Message on Day 3

Oh, my beautiful Victoria. I know it's been hard for you to release all my stuff that I accumulated over 15 years. I am sorry. Your efforts are noted and will result in something amazingly positive. There will be an unexpected shift and clarity will be obvious.

I am working on bringing you an equally generous man who will love and accept you as you are. You needed to experience the contrast so you will not settle for what doesn't work for you. What we had together was very special. I am forever grateful for the time we shared together and for the *ways you supported me and championed me towards the end of my earthly life. I have not forgotten.*

The next thing I want to share with you is of a more personal nature. I have learned many things about my personality Bernie (Bernhard) Klein—many of which I am proud of and many not so much. The things I am most proud of are my children who I miss a lot. Be sure to tell them so. I am proud of how I cared for other people and would do just about anything to help them.

I am not so proud that I put others before me and my own life. As you know, all the millions of things in the backyard, front yard, side yards and inside everywhere, were to represent how much love I wanted and needed. What I didn't take advantage of was all the love you had for me, which was greater than all those things combined. I missed out on experiencing even more love because I couldn't see or feel anything—there was no room. It's amazing how fast you've let go of so much. As you continue to declutter, it'll make more time to just be and to go have more fun. Keep dancing. Go even when you don't feel like it, even if it's for a short time. Just go for the fun of it. I know it feeds your soul like singing and writing.

As for Robert—what a gift! He kept his promise to help you keep the house. Your office looks stunning. Yes, with a lot of work, the whole house could be renovated to be the home you wanted. More on that later.

Back to me. I am proud of the way I loved you the best way I knew how with my shortcomings. I can see now I was unable to please you in the area you wanted the most, intimacy— spending time sharing and just being with one another. The thing I am not so proud of was my stubbornness and lack of taking action. I can see now how it affected many people around me, including and foremost you.

I am seeing now that the very thing I wanted from you I wasn't giving you—quality time for sharing and being more transparent. There is nothing hidden anymore. As I mentioned before, I am continuing to look in the mirror. I wasted a lot of time playing poker and watching movies late into the night, rather than look in the mirror and take action on the millions of items you are now taking care of on my behalf, for which I am eternally grateful. There is a greater plan that will be very beneficial for you. Don't give up. Keep going. Robert will help, you'll see. Please reach out to Dunny again, he'll be helping too.

This is enough for today—I love you, Victoria. Until tomorrow, know I love you with all my heart.

Message on Day 4

Good morning my sweet beloved Victoria. There is so much I want to say about so many things. After my project in Hawaii, we'll talk again. Mark it on your calendar and be ready.

I have a message for Robert. Hey bro—I miss you! You were right about a lot of things. Mostly I want to thank you for being such a great friend. I could say anything, and you'd hang in there with me. Thank you for taking care of my wife. She's a gem. Her office looks spectacular! Your attention to detail is amazing. I am doing well, mostly. I apologize for being so stubborn especially when it came to releasing my shit that YOU have been releasing on my behalf and for Victoria. Your efforts are noted and appreciated beyond measure. Please consider taking the van for your transportation for all your efforts. I know what you mean now, about the different densities— more on that later. Take care of yourself man.

Back to you Victoria. I want to take responsibility for all the ways I caused you hurt. I was downright lazy and cheap. Any type of forward movement was your doing, and many times, your encouragement was followed by my resistance and flat-out NO. I know how severely my financial lifestyle affected you. I could tell you lost respect for me, so I tried to earn it back with all my spiritual mumbo jumbo. The truth is you are a bright light. Do not let anyone dim you ever. I let you shine as much as I could handle and for that I also apologize. With a foundation of a beautiful home, you could have soared even more.

It's amazing how much work you have accomplished in the house. Like I said previously, there will be a surprise event and clarity will come on whether to stay or leave. It's your choice. Do not let me influence your decision. Don't stay to hold on to what we shared there. Take me in your heart wherever you go. You don't need to stay there. The next man will shower you with even more than the last one—allow, allow, allow. You deserve the best. I must go now. I love you my sweet Victoria.

Message on Day 5

My dearest Victoria, I'm sorry I'm late in your linear time. I never was good with that. This time I was finishing up training and teaching stuck souls some options for their growth and development. Some were eager to hear and take action and others had no interest. It's not really that different from humans on earth.

Today I want to speak of love. It is such a limiting word actually—being and accepting are similar words. Love is not something you look for—it is who you are. It is who everyone is. You did a great job explaining this in your book, **What Would Love Do Right Now? A Guide to Living an Extraordinary**

Life. I am so proud you got it out the very week after I left. It's important in your work with people that you remind them that love is who they are, especially in your group that is focusing on intimate relationships. Another topic is kindness. My friend Steve had it right all along. Kindness Rules! Begin first with yourself, then others.

As the anniversary of my liberation comes closer, take time to evaluate what Victoria wants—how she wants to live, where she wants to live, and with whom, if anyone. The silence is precious. Do what feeds your soul always. Call on Bruno Groening. He really wants to help you, even if it's five minutes in the morning and five minutes before bed. Let's take the next five minutes in silence so we can feel each other. I am always with you.

Continue to be really good to yourself. Have fun, go out, be yourself. Don't be so hard on yourself and keep moving forward with this book. It is needed and wanted. The people who need it will find it. You can use it when you speak to hospice groups. Mikelle will help you get connected. I go now. We'll reconvene the day before the anniversary of my liberation.

I am blessed to have known you and to be loved by you! I love you, Victoria.

Awesome—five messages in a row! I felt closer to my beloved than ever. It took several days to digest Bernie's communication. I reached out to Carol and Lynette in Hawaii, as he requested. They both agreed to meditate on the success of his mission there—I also did the same. It's funny, before he even mentioned it, I had been thinking about speaking at hospice locations after I publish this book—good confirmation. Speaking of confirmation, his messages provided lots of it, especially as it pertained to our love, which will forever be in my heart.

Along with everything else that was happening, I continued to see clients, which always fulfilled my desire to have a positive impact in the lives of others. In October, I facilitated a 5-week proxy group repatterning series called, *Feel Free to Love and Be Loved,* for eight clients. My clients really liked these groups because they didn't need to come in person and they could still get the full benefits. It was very impactful for the participants because they got to release old hurts, betrayals, disappointments, negative attitudes, and conclusions that were influencing the relationships they were in or preventing them from having the ones they wanted. Did I tell you I love the transformational sessions I do?

The Unity Church Business Fair was held on November 4. I loved this event. It was smaller than other ones I participated in and only lasted four hours. Since I didn't need help with supplies and setup, I was able to get everything packed and ready the previous morning. I was excited to share with the parishioners my #1 bestselling book. I could hardly wait to tell them about repatterning and the positive difference it could make in their lives. Before the event started, I walked around to the other booths to introduce myself and exchange business cards—it was great to meet the other business owners and share information and tips.

I donated a personal repatterning session and one of my books to the fair's raffle. I also created a personal raffle of these same items at my booth for people who provided their business card or contact information. About 150 people entered my raffle, the prize winners were well pleased. Besides meeting other business owners and potential clients, I sold a few books. Yay! Although I missed Bernie being with me, I knew he was looking down on me, saying, *"You Go Girl!"*

In mid-November, my mom and I took a drive up to Sedona. We enjoyed taking in the stunning red-rock scenery we loved, which brought back pleasant memories of our trips in the past—we had done this many times during our years living in Arizona. She bought me a truly meaningful calendar for 2019 titled, *To a Beautiful, Outstanding Woman.* Each month had an inspirational quote. She took her time and looked at every calendar, then said, *"This is the one I want you to have."* It was the last heartfelt gift I received from her as her awareness dimmed. I still read these messages every month.

Two days later, when Carmen went over to check on my mom, she found her face down on the floor in the living room. She called an ambulance. When the paramedics got there, mom refused to go with them. They suggested Carmen give her a dose of her medication, which she did. After they left, she called me, and I drove over. Mom was livid! *"I'm not going anywhere with strange men!"* I was so frustrated and at a loss about what to do.

Carmen and I then came up with a solution—put mom's medication in a small cash box and keep it at Carmen's house. This would make it easier for us to know whether she was taking one and only one dose a day. This time, my mom went along with this idea. Yes! The next morning, she stormed over to Carmen's and demanded the box, saying that she could manage taking her pills herself—surprise, surprise. We were back to square one.

It was my first Thanksgiving without Bernie. That morning, I went for a long walk through the park near my house, which always made me happy. Thoughts of all of our celebrations together, which were both comforting and bittersweet, flooded my mind and heart. That afternoon I visited my girlfriend Karri, then dinner at Michael and Patti's place. I brought wine and everyone's favorite—my Brussels sprouts with toasted sesame oil and home-roasted sesame seeds. It was special being around people who loved and cared about me. Once again, it felt so odd being there without Bernie.

Sure enough, on November 26, the day before the first anniversary of

Bernie's liberation, I received another message from him—I could hardly believe one year had already passed. Here is what he had to tell me.

Oh, my sweet, sweet Victoria, you know not of your beauty. Feel my arms around you. Feel my love for you. There is not a day in your linear time that I don't think about you and relish in the love we shared and still share. I know it's been tough for you some days. You have done so well in your transition without me physically at your side. As you reminisce about our life together, let it fill your heart with love, then take that love and fill yourself first then give to others. The right man is on his way to love and accept you just the way you are, and who is ready for a big love like you give. Stay tuned. For now, love the ones you're with!

My time in the Hawaiian Islands was successful. Now I am off to Cambodia. I will be in different regions of the earth to continue to repair the energy grids. I asked for a way to make up for my mess on earth that you are cleaning up ever so thoroughly and quickly in linear time. As you evaluate, remember that you don't have to stay there as a way to honor or remember me and our love. That energy is within you. Take that love and spread it. My service will be over the next six months in your linear time. I will be in contact with you two more times during these six months.

As for Robert, thank him for me for all the ways he served me and the ways he challenged me. I will only be in touch with him through you. After my six months, I will be going to a different density, only to return when you liberate your soul.

The energy here is fluid and quick—you ask and you receive. If I was to give you any guidance, it would be to remember to ask more often. Continue to reach out to your

current clients to remind them of the opportunity they have
to free themselves of patterns that don't work for them. All is
well—you will see. There is an opportunity coming your way
in January. You would be wise to accept.

I love you dearly. Thank you for all the ways you love me.
I became a better man because of your love. I must go now.

Your Beloved Bernie.

My inner response to Bernie's message was—cool, a big love is on its way. It feels too soon, although I do miss loving someone special and being loved in return. Time will tell. Right now, I miss loving Bernie. I'm also eager to find out about the opportunity that is coming my way in January.

The next day I reflected on how far I'd come in my grief process in just one year. Yes, I had my moments of sadness and anger, however, mostly my life was full of joy, even with cleaning up after Bernie and all of my other projects. It had been a while since I saw a penny in my path, this time there was one on the side table by the chair where I was sitting. I took Bernie's picture and held it close to my heart, which helped me feel his love. Love you, Bernie.

December 12, I went to an Equinoxx channeling session and Bernie came through with another message. This is what Joan received from him.

You don't need to shout. I am fine, very fine. The transition
was total expansion, every aspect of flowers. It's like a lens on
a camera, everywhere I looked there was beauty—beauty all
around. Every time I thought of someone, they would appear
right in front of me.

It's so important to watch what you are thinking and
saying and be careful what you say you want. The veils are
getting thinner, and manifestations can occur faster than
blinking your eye. There is truth to the concept that we reap
what we sow. All deeds are noted and depending on what it

is, you will experience the consequence. Be oh so gentle with yourselves.

Oh, my beloved Victoria, I love you so. I am with you always. Thank you so much for all you did to make my transition smooth. I will be in touch.

Your Beloved Bernie

This was a gentle reminder to get clear on what I wanted and watch what I thought and said to myself and others. I feel your loving presence Bernie. Thank you! I realized how much I valued and felt my connection to him and our love for each other, which strengthened me in moments of sadness. I also understood from his messages that I would hear from him less frequently, yet knew I would always carry his communications and love in my heart.

Every once in a while, when I was having one of my moments of missing Bernie, I wondered if I should join a grief group—instead I'd pick up the phone and call my friend, Linda. If she wasn't available, I kept reaching out until I found someone to listen to me. The conversations didn't take long. I just needed to be heard and reassured that I was doing fine and to feel my feelings as they surfaced. My friends told me the same thing I would tell my clients. It was comforting to be on the receiving end of others' loving support.

Just before Christmas, I was sitting on the couch and got up to make some lunch. Unfortunately, when I stood up, my ankle buckled under me— OUCH. I iced it, elevated it, took something for the pain, limped around the house the rest of the day, and had a restless night's sleep. In the morning, it was clear I needed a doctor's opinion. I took myself to Urgent Care where they did an x-ray—not broken, just a bad sprain! They wrapped it and gave me a prescription for weekly physical therapy sessions. No holiday dancing for me. Merry Christmas?

The day before Christmas eve, I went to visit Christopher. We had lunch, played cards, and recalled all the delightful times we shared with Bernie— we had a great visit. Since he lived close to my mom, I stopped to see her afterward.

I found mom confused and disoriented, and her house was a mess again. With my sprained ankle, I did the best I could to straighten up and clean out the litter box, while answering her questions about what was happening to her mind. Every time I saw her, she understandably wanted to visit a doctor about her brain. I reminded her she had been to the doctor the previous week, and that she had an upcoming doctor's appointment on Thursday. She pulled out her guilt card and said, *"If you really loved me, you'd make sure I got to a doctor today!"* I let her know it was Sunday, and the doctor was not available. She refused to believe me and insisted that I was making it all up, so that I could go home instead of taking care of her. There was no reasoning with her. I felt the need to shield myself from her hurtful comments for my own well-being. I did my best to put myself in her shoes—I'm sure I wouldn't want to lose my independence either. I got through it by keeping in mind that it was the dementia talking, not my mom. We had dinner in silence and I left.

Christmas morning, I drove over again, only to find my mom remarkably disoriented and the house even messier than it had been two days before. She had forgotten it was Christmas and questioned why I was there again—she kept telling me she was fine, she could handle her life, and that I should stop meddling and mind my own business! Even though this behavior was difficult to handle, I was able to keep in mind what was happening to her, stay connected, and not react negatively.

Carmen came over to check in and to give mom her medication. We hoped she had not already taken it, so we weren't doubling her dose. It was great to see Carmen. I thanked her profusely and gave her a Christmas card with a cash bonus for all the care she was providing to my mom. She humbly said it was a joy and blessing to help her friend.

After Carmen left, mom and I had a delicious relaxing breakfast. Time for gifts. When she realized it was Christmas and she hadn't bought me a present, she was totally embarrassed. I had thought she might forget what day it was, so I brought a gift for me from her, just in case. I handed her the present for me, which made her feel better—then we exchanged our Christmas gifts. She again wanted me to take her to the doctor as soon as possible—I reminded her that she had an appointment in two days. I straightened up a bit, then off I went to have dinner with my friends.

On my way to Michael and Patti's house, I realized her behavior was unmistakable evidence that she was going downhill rapidly. I knew the day was swiftly approaching when something more serious would happen, which would finally allow her to receive the care she desperately needed. That day came sooner than I thought it might.

Two days later, I showed up early at my mom's, making sure we'd be on time for her doctor's appointment. She informed me she had canceled the appointment. I lost it!

"Why didn't you call me? I took off work to go with you. You keep telling me you want to go the doctor, I make an appointment for you, then you cancel it! I have had it with you!"

She shouted back, *"You're not in charge of my life—I am. I can do what I want, when I want, and you can't do a thing about it!"*

While she continued to insult me and tell me I was a bad daughter, I walked outside to cool off. I kept reminding myself that her mind was deteriorating and that the words coming out of her mouth at me were not coherent thoughts. Even though the social worker warned me that this would happen, and I knew it was coming, I wasn't prepared. After calming down, I went back in and her face was red as a beet! When I asked her if she had taken her medication, she said, *"Of course I did."* Then, I called Carmen to check. She told me she had given mom her medicine earlier. I gave my mom some water and called the doctor's office to tell them what had happened—they gave us an appointment for 1:00.

We were civil to each other on the drive over. When we arrived, she was slurring her words, talking incoherently, and her blood pressure was off the charts! Off to the ER we went again. This time, she stayed overnight for observation. I was exhausted and about to give up! It took every ounce of will power I had to finally let her fail so she could get the support she needed.

I drove back to the hospital after my morning client to be there to take her home, when she was discharged. The doctor, who released her, insisted that she should no longer live alone. My mom declared she wasn't moving anywhere, and she could take care of herself without anyone's interference!

After talking to the doctor at the hospital, I took action immediately— scheduling two home visit appointments for January 2. One, in the morning, with a social worker to determine if she qualified for in-home healthcare; and another, in the afternoon, with a nurse from Arizona Long Term Care (ALTC), to evaluate her medical status for assisted living approval. She already qualified financially, and hopefully this would qualify her medically. The appointments were only a couple of hours apart, which meant I would only need to make the drive to Mesa once.

Inasmuch as I would have enjoyed going to a semi-formal dance party on New Year's Eve, my sprained ankle kept me home—bummer. Sitting there on my couch, elevating my foot, I had the opportunity to look back over the year and acknowledge how perfectly the intentions I created for my business and my life had manifested. My major accomplishments were moving into my home office and having my published eBook reach Amazon #1 bestseller status. I attributed my success to being able to live my life without the overwhelming grief of being a widow. I remained grateful for my capacity to leave nothing unsaid between Bernie and I before he passed. I realized that during the last months of Bernie's life, I allowed myself to really grieve what was inevitable, so when he actually passed, I was relieved and happy for him. This made my adjustment to not having Bernie by my side smoother, taking the necessary actions to move forward easier. I wasn't distraught, so I had the energy to create a grand new life.

At 10:00, midnight in New York City, I sat in my living room enjoying the Times Square Ball Drop on TV. What a year!

The Year of Transition

The year began with moving my mom into an assisted living facility. My major concerns for the next several months were sorting and selling her assets, managing her finances, and helping her acclimate to a whole new environment—that she fought tooth and nail!

My ankle injury made the first two months of 2019 very inconvenient. I had to take time out of my busy life to sit still and elevate my foot, which allowed me to catch up on my reading. It was torture not being able to dance while I was healing. When I resumed dancing every week, my dance peeps were glad to see me, and it felt wonderful to be doing what I was passionate about again—I was so happy.

Along with working with clients and promoting my published book, I added securing a referral source and facilitating four proxy groups to my business goals.

January 2 came, the day I had been both anticipating and dreading. I drove out to my mom's early in the morning, sprained ankle and all, to make sure I was with her during her home-visit appointments. What happened that day must have been divinely orchestrated. When I arrived, my mom was slurring her words and not making any sense. When the social worker got there, she saw that my mother was totally incoherent and determined she was in the midst of a delusional episode. The ALTC nurse showed up two hours later and concluded that my mother's level of disorientation medically qualified her, on the spot, for admission to an in-patient facility for evaluation and future long-term care.

The social worker secured her a place at a memory care unit for evaluation. I was frightened, yet relieved, that my mom could now receive the services she needed. Although my mother had become slightly more coherent, we concluded that having an ambulance come to pick her up would most likely increase her agitation. The social worker suggested I take her to lunch, make up a story about wanting her to meet a friend of mine in downtown Phoenix, and then drive her to the facility myself. I hated to deceive her like that, however, I couldn't figure out any other way to get her there. If I'd been honest and told her what was happening, she wouldn't have even gotten in the car.

At first, it worked. When mom and I arrived, I hugged the nurse and introduced her to my mom as my friend. She bought it for a while until seeing several people in the main room who were obviously ill. She started yelling at me, saying I had tricked her, that she didn't belong there, and demanding to be taken home. After I finished the paperwork, the admitting nurse suggested that I sneak out the back door and reassured me that my mother would be fine. I chose to trust the nurse and followed her instructions. Driving home, I felt somewhat guilty for the deception, yet I knew that what I had done was ultimately good for my mother, and no matter how I got her there, she was safe. I could now breathe easier knowing she was being cared for.

The doctor at the memory care unit did several cognitive tests and deemed my mother incapable of making her own life choices. A week after being admitted, she was discharged from the in-patient facility and transferred to an assisted living center that was about ten minutes from my place. As you may imagine, my mother was livid. *"What about my cats? Where are my clothes? Who's watching my house?"* I told her Carmen was gladly taking caring of the cats and the house. Mom didn't believe me. I wondered if this was the opportunity Bernie was talking about in his message in November— it definitely was a way to relieve myself of the stress and worry that had been my constant companion during the past year.

A few weeks later, a nursing assistant from the facility called me to ask if it was okay if my mom smoked. Although I was shocked and didn't really think it was a great idea, I said yes. She had been a non-smoker for over 30 years. I wondered if her dementia was taking her back to old habits? I thought perhaps she started smoking again as a way to demonstrate her independence. Was she going back to smoking a pack a day? That's exactly what she did.

Near the end of January, Bruce and Rochelle, my brother and sister, came down from Wisconsin for a week to help me settle our mother's estate. All of us and the social worker visited mom and explained why Bruce and Rochelle were in town and what we were planning to do. She started yelling and insisting she was leaving. I understood her reaction as she'd been independent her entire life and now, her home, her car, her cats, and everything else were being taken away. All that in addition to being in an unfamiliar environment with a bunch of strangers. She insisted that we all leave and never come back. We were disowned! I didn't expect that, especially since mom hadn't seen my brother and sister for a couple of years. They did not visit her again before going home. The lack of appreciation for all the ways I supported her over the past few years was hurtful. At the same time, I knew she was struggling in her fight for independence, and did my best not to take her words personally. I waited three weeks before going back to see her.

I was grateful and relieved that my brother and sister were here to help get our mom's affairs in order. I took a week off from seeing clients and we got a lot accomplished before they left. We dropped her cats off at the Humane Society, sold her car, and went through every room, releasing all the items mom wouldn't need in her new place. We started in the laundry area with the cat's litter box—it was toxic, I could hardly go in! It was much easier to tackle the rest of the house after we cleaned that mess.

We called our sister, Denise, to ask what she wanted, and we each took a few keepsakes. I loaded at least 20 boxes of photo albums, clothing, shoes, and essential paperwork into my car to go through later. Jerry, another one of my mother's neighbors, created Craig's List, Offer-Up, and Facebook Marketplace posts for some of her furniture and valuable items. He also put her home up for sale on social media and unlocked it whenever people came to view it, so I didn't have to drive over. By the end of the month, we sold her house and most of the furniture—terrific! Jerry took what was left in the house to the Purple Heart Desert Thrift Shop, which assists Veterans and people in crisis. He was definitely one of my heroes!

My first visit, after our mother had thrown us all out of her room, went better than I thought it might. When she asked about when I was going to take her home, I reminded her that her doctor said she could no longer live alone, so we sold her house and car. She was still upset, but civil. I didn't mention the cats and surprisingly, she didn't either.

With a few exceptions, I spent every Friday and Saturday working with Betsy on expanding my transformational healing business through website and social media activity. I worked with many clients throughout the year, and it brought me considerable satisfaction to know I was continuing my mission to support each of them in aligning with their goals and dreams.

I gave a ZOOM presentation called, *Got a Nudge to Write?* to the Repatterning Practitioner's Association in early February, which I had prepared while getting my mom settled. I received feedback from a few participants, letting me know it had inspired them to begin the book they had been putting off for years. How cool is that?

During the first half of the year, I led two proxy groups. I started with *Live a Purpose Driven Life* for eight clients over five weeks. They identified a dream worth living for and aligned with optimal health and well-being, financial freedom, romance in their heart, and being fully self-expressed. I then began my *Realize Ideal Happiness* group, that lasted 10 weeks and was all about balancing the Chakra system, making available to each person the positive qualities associated with each Chakra. The seven participants dramatically improved their well-being and joy in many areas of their lives. Again, these sessions were popular because the participants didn't have to leave the privacy of their home to get the benefits they wanted.

I had been hoping a new year would bring a new man and, sure enough, it did—eventually. After my ankle healed and I could dance again, I reconnected with Steve, who introduced me to Contra dancing—square dancing on steroids. We went to events in Phoenix, Socorro, NM, and San Jose, CA. We even performed a flash mob routine at the AZ Classic Country Dance event.

I opened my heart a little more with Steve. He was a nice and generous man. We had some fabulous dinners, took a hot-air balloon ride, had fun at the circus, and attended several outdoor concerts. He had season tickets at Gammage Auditorium, where we saw several outstanding shows. We also volunteered to usher at the Phoenix Theatre and watched some plays for free.

In July, while Steve and I were in San Jose for a week-long contra dance function, I visited my Uncle Mark and Aunt Pam. It had been a while since we had seen each other, so it was wonderful spending time with them.

Even though we had lots of good times together, it had become clear to me that I was not in love with Steve. Some of his habits and beliefs wouldn't work for me in the long run, and I broke up with him shortly after we returned from San Jose.

We had developed a solid friendship along the way, and I was hoping to remain friends. In the beginning, he also wanted that, then he changed his mind. This was especially hard for me because he was such a good friend, and it took a while for me to recover.

Heartbreak number two. I learned how important it was for me that my romantic partner have a spiritual foundation guiding his life that we could share and celebrate.

Time for more releasing and organizing. My friends Mimi and Angela had come over on New Year's Day and spent hours with me releasing Bernie's things from the back patio—at first, we couldn't even see the tile. It was wall to wall, junk. When we finished trashing his treasures, I was astonished to discover I had a huge 10-foot wide, floor-to-ceiling window streaming light into my living room. What a way to bring in the new year!

Starting in March, Paula spent four or five days a month for the next six months working with me to release more from the apartment. We moved enough stuff out of the way in the foyer to make it easier to take things out the door. We cleared out the kitchen area so I could actually open the drawers to the file cabinets in that space. At one point, I realized I could finally see the living room floor and could spread out to pack multiple boxes at a time for donation.

There were piles of papers everywhere—Bernie's, my mom's, and even a few of my own. I hardly knew where to begin! OMG, Bernie kept every piece of paper he got over the past fifteen or twenty years—most of which were useless. Going through the file cabinets, folder by folder, page by page, was tedious. I was eventually rewarded with CASH—lucky me! I also trimmed down my mom's paperwork from two stuffed banker's boxes to a single accordion file—perfect. Next, my personal files. I was a bit surprised I had saved so many brochures and flyers about travel, conferences, and dance events, all of which were out of date. I eliminated about 70% of the paperwork I had been saving for years.

My sister Denise visited from Wisconsin in May for a long weekend to sort through and release what we could from our mother's personal belongings that I had brought home. I asked my sister when she'd like to visit mom. She was hesitant at first, because of what had happened when she visited after mom's surgery in 2017. It was clear that mom had forgotten all about that episode, even though it still weighed heavily on Denise's heart. We went to the Center for a brief time every day and she was so happy to see us.

Given that I still had so many of Bernie's things cluttering my space, I wanted to remove as much of mom's stuff as possible. We made a lot of progress and donated what I wasn't keeping to The Salvation Army. By the time Denise left, there were only eight boxes remaining that I eventually sorted through.

In mid-August, I took a break from clearing the clutter and traveled to Albuquerque to visit Rudrani, then up to Santa Fe to spend time with

Donna. My favorite dance fiesta event was the following month, so back to Albuquerque I went and Donna met me there. We delighted in each other's company and danced the nights away!

Mimi and Angela returned in October. It was time to clear out all the kitchen cabinets; clean the refrigerator; throw away outdated condiments, spices, and food staples; and get rid of old towels, sheets, blankets, and table clothes from the linen closet. Then we started on the boxes stacked in the corner of the patio containing my belongings from my condo that I could now unpack. We eliminated what I no longer wanted and sorted what was left. Finally, I was ready to move my pots and pans, dishes, glassware, cooking utensils, coffee maker, linens, pictures, nick-nacks, and extra clothes in and claim the house as my own. I had a deep sense of accomplishment and satisfaction.

At the end of October, I attended a 2-day motivational business success workshop in Phoenix where I met four remarkable businesswomen. We started weekly Fab Five ZOOM gatherings. After a short check-in, one of us would do a 15- to 20-minute talk on a subject that could benefit everyone— my turn came every fifth week. We all were published authors, coaches, or transformational healing practitioners, so we presented concepts from a book we had written or were reading, or anything we wanted to share from our practice. After the presentation, we each reported on our progress meeting the goals we set previously and created new intentions for the upcoming week. We ended our meetings with sharing our greatness—each woman identified a positive personal quality they had experienced since we last met. It was encouraging to have one another's accountability, and we all appreciated each other's contribution. I genuinely enjoyed being able to impact these women by expressing my wisdom, and I learned so much from them while expanding my network of support. It was inspiring.

In September and November, I led two more proxy groups, each scheduled for four weeks. *Clearing Your Limiting Beliefs Around Money* with 21 participants, helped them discover and release their negative thought patterns about money and align with their financial goals for success. *Clearing the Limiting Beliefs Around People* with 15 participants, focused on restoring harmony within themselves and with their friends, relatives, sweethearts, and associates—ultimately, to fulfill their desire to love and be loved by those who were special in their life.

As part of my ongoing professional education and growth, I attended a 4-day virtual course in late October. It was very informative, and I was introduced to several transformational processes that I quickly implemented with my clients.

In the beginning of November, I once again took part in the annual Unity of Phoenix Business Fair. I always enjoyed this event because I could interact closely with other business owners and, most importantly, with potential clients and readers. More book sales. Yay!

An exciting development happened in my business in mid-November. One of my clients told her spiritual counselor about the significant results she was having with me. Dawn Eagle Woman contacted me and I gave her a complimentary session, which she loved. She started sending me people who were interested in my work—the new referral source I intended to attract fell right into my lap. I was ecstatic.

Thanksgiving morning, I picked up my mom and drove her to my place. I enjoyed making her a special breakfast and she was very appreciative to be with me, away from the Center. After I took her back and made sure she was settled in, I went to Granada Park for a long walk and fed the ducks at both ponds. Next, I was off to a wonderful dinner with several friends at Michael and Patti's home. When I left a few hours later, I was still stuffed!

On the second anniversary of Bernie's liberation, I took his photo and held it close to my heart and thanked him for all the love we shared. His love enhanced my capacity to open my heart, love myself, and fully express my love to those around me. I soaked in the fond memories and let them flood my body and my soul. And yes, another penny, this time next to my computer where I wouldn't miss it. I feel your presence Bernie. I love you!

I received two messages from Bernie this year—by way of emails—from Dawn Katar, who channels daily *Point of Peace Messages from The Ascended Realms* to inspire and nurture peace.

Message #1 on September 5

"*Want more Peace? Be nice. Smile. You can bring more peace to your awareness as you bring it to the world©.*" *~Ascended Master Bernie.*

Message #2 on December 6

"*Some think that they are the center of the Universe. Perhaps your center is where the Universe resides. If you think of yourself as the center of the Universe, you will be efforting to control or to vision what seems to be outside of yourself. When you understand the Universe is within, you will be able to know and understand that you have nothing to control. All is You. You are All©.*" *~Ascended Master Bernie.*

It was such a surprise when I opened these emails, and the message was from Bernie. Both were exactly what I thought he would say—they warmed my heart and I again felt our deep connection. These timely messages could not have been more welcoming as I headed into the holiday season missing Bernie and creating new traditions with new adventures.

The first week of December, I attended a meditation retreat in Cancun, Mexico, where I met Allen. He was from Canada and oddly not a dancer.

I had given myself five months to heal from my previous heartbreak, so I thought it was time to get back into the swing of things. He joined a friend and me for dinner the first couple of evenings, then we dined alone. He told me he was divorced and his conversation indicated to me he was ready to move on. More to come in the new year—wondering how a long-distance relationship would work.

Christmas Eve at Unity Church with two of my friends was totally uplifting. It brought back sacred memories of sitting there with Bernie holding hands, enjoying the service. I realized that I was doing quite well without him there with me because he was in my heart wherever I went.

On Christmas Day, I visited my mom, and we opened presents—she was always glad to see me. It was much easier to maintain our connection since she now lived close to me. Afterward, I spent time with my friend Karri and her boyfriend, who I hadn't seen in a while. We shared a savory meal and had lots of laughs.

At the end of the year, I mailed my sister, Denise, all the family photos, which she agreed to sort and designate some to each of us kids. I felt relieved that there was one less project on my plate. Thank you, Sis!

Reviewing my business goals for my second year after Bernie's death, I had some insights about what had occurred without me noticing. I realized how much I had accomplished through all the programs and workshops, vendor booths, and speaking engagements I did for both my readers and my clients. Having a new referral source began to increase my client base, which was incredibly gratifying.

Although I hadn't been as active as I intended in promoting my book—book sales still happened. After discussions with Betsy and Paula, I chose to set aside my two Fairy Realm books until I completed writing a third book to create a trilogy. This gave me the chance to begin work on revising another book I had written titled, *Three Magical Words for a Magical Life.*

Transitioning my mother's living situation to ensure she received the care she needed, altered what had been a burden for me—to the gift of being able to fully express the deep love I have for her. I love you, Mom.

What an exhilarating year! The last day of 2019, I attended a dance party, which was a marvelous way to bring in 2020!

The Year of Transformation

Time was flying by quickly. It was now 2020 and hard to believe Bernie had been gone for over two years. I did my best to focus on the good times we shared, which kept me going. Deep in my heart I knew he wanted me to live a full life again, so I was doing just that!

I visited my mom at the Center or brought her to my house about once a month. We played cards, looked through family photos, and reminisced about things she remembered—she often expressed her gratitude for my visits. When I took her out, she genuinely enjoyed the ride and the change of scenery. Usually she didn't want to go back at all. I also made sure to see her on special occasions like our birthdays, Mother's Day, Thanksgiving, and Christmas. When family or friends sent gifts, I would bring her thank you cards and write what she wanted to say, then she would sign them, and I would put them in the mail.

Once again, I reviewed my business goals from the previous year. My additional intentions for this year were to increase the number of clients I served and prepare the second book I intended to publish.

I started my business year off by leading my four-session, *Clear Your Limiting Beliefs Around Well-Being,* proxy group to 12 participants. This series was designed to release negative beliefs on the physical, emotional, mental, and spiritual levels in order to experience more vitality, joy, clarity, and affinity.

I also facilitated my ten-session, *Raise Your Vibration—Lower Your Weight,* proxy group at the end of March and again in October. Each group had six participants who cleared their limiting beliefs around the types of food to eat; when to eat; how much to eat; how fast to eat; and how frequently to eat. This freed the clients to make lifestyle changes that were consistent with super-health and vitality that naturally lead to reaching their optimal weight.

A new year with a new man. Yes! I had a short, long-distance relationship with Allen, whom I had met in Cancun. He visited me twice in January and we had a blast! We had so much in common and he spoke so sincerely of wanting to deepen our connection, I thought for sure we'd stay in touch. Then, two weeks after his last visit, no email, no calls, no nothing—I had no idea what was happening. A friend told me I'd been ghosted. OUCH! I had genuinely opened my heart to him, so this breakup hurt the most.

Heartbreak number three. I realized I forgot to check-in with my own rule about divorce and rebound relationships. I truly wanted a romantic partner who was not on the rebound—someone who had been out of a major relationship for at least a year.

Bernie had sent me the message to love again and said he would find me a great guy—it wasn't working so far. Yikes Stripes Bernie, you're sending me all the wrong guys.

I resumed clearing out and releasing Bernie's treasures, bit-by-bit. I even took an assortment of equipment to a sports consignment store. Unfortunately, none of it was in good enough shape for them to sell. Everything was donated, discarded, or kept to sell later.

On the last Friday in March, I went to a group channeling with Torina. I had already moved on from my relationship with Bernie and was wondering why that special man hadn't shown up. Right before the session ended, Bernie came through loud and clear.

I am so sorry Victoria for holding you back from your next
true love and not releasing you sooner. I am ready now. It's time

for me to go on my next journey. I now set you free, and I set myself free. I love you and always will. Again, I am sorry.

It warmed my heart to hear from Bernie and helped me understand why I hadn't found the right man yet. This communication was the last one I've received—I don't expect direct contact with him again. After hearing his message, setting me free, I felt even more open to love and to be loved. I was eager to put myself out there as available. That proved to be a little hard to do.

2020 was suddenly divided into pre-/post-pandemic. When we reached lockdown status in April, everything changed. When dance lessons were on hold, it just about killed my spirit, but I didn't let it—almost every week my friend Larry Joe (LJ), my primary west coast swing partner, stopped by and we danced in my kitchen. I also did my best to maintain my self-care routines at home.

I switched as many other activities as I could to ZOOM and the phone—the Higher Vibrations choir; my in-person repatterning groups; my individual sessions; and my business continuing education classes. The Fab Five had always been on ZOOM, so we were set to keep on track with our goals.

At the Raise Your Vibration ZOOM event, hosted by Howard Chait in May, I presented the practical principles from my Amazon #1 bestselling book, *What Would Love Do Right Now?* Then I facilitated a transformational healing session for the participants using my *Inquiry to Resolution* process. It was an amazing opportunity to make a difference in the lives of the people who attended and those who will listen to the recording.

During the pandemic, I got extremely creative when visiting my mom at the assisted living facility. Rules were strict. They wouldn't let me inside the facility and I couldn't take her out anywhere. To solve the problem, I moved a patio table and chair from the courtyard to the fence and then took another chair outside the fence so we could sit across from each other to talk and play cards. People who came to deliver supplies often commented on our desire to make sure we could spend time together and how imaginative we were.

At the beginning of the lockdown, my friend Christopher's extended trip out of the country was postponed indefinitely, and he needed a place to stay. I rented Bernie's room to him for a few months before he moved to Pine, AZ. This arrangement was perfect as I had a bit of money coming in and he helped me with some home projects I had going. He evaluated a myriad of camping equipment, the portable air conditioner, and some small appliances to determine if they worked and whether they should be kept or released. In the front yard, he also arranged decorative pavers under the spigot. Besides the personal connection, it was healthy for my pocketbook that I had a friend who needed a short-term place to live.

I took full advantage of the extra time made available by the lockdown to sort, organize, and release more of Bernie's treasures, as well as my own belongings and files. The biggest job was clearing out yet another accumulation of sports shoes, bug traps, and other assorted rubbish from the dilapidated cabinet on the back patio.

By April, I was ready for a new love. During the pandemic we were encouraged to stay home, and the dance studios were closed. I tried online dating instead—I'd never done it before. It sounded like a good idea—WRONG! The men I was matched with were passive, no asking for a virtual date, no follow-through, no nothin'—how frustrating and disappointing.

Remember Allen from Canada? It surprised me when he contacted me, out of the blue. He sincerely apologized for withdrawing so suddenly, without telling me why. He promised not to do that again and asked if we could resume getting to know each other better—I agreed. We FaceTimed for a couple of months—then…ghosted again! I was angry and felt betrayed that he had not kept his promise.

Despite everything, I remained open in the relationship department and did not give up. I still knew I was headed for another grand love—someday!

The most profound experience I had during 2020 happened on July 9. Over the year and a half I had known LJ, we had many philosophical conversations in which he often mentioned his personal connection with Jesus—leaving subtle breadcrumbs for me to follow. On this particular evening, I listened in a new way to what I was hearing.

My father was a Catholic, and we were raised in that faith until he moved out. I never had a deep spiritual relationship with Jesus, and I didn't understand what LJ meant when he asked, *"Have you ever considered accepting Jesus Christ as your Lord and Savior?"*

What popped out of my mouth shocked me. *"No, he took my daddy from me!"* Wow, that must have been somewhere in the recesses of my unconscious mind. I told him about where I thought that answer came from.

> *When I was a little girl, my dad was my spiritual mentor. He and I would pray together at night, and he'd read me Bible stories—it was our special time. When I was 12, my mother asked my father for a divorce. Even though he didn't want that, he left our home at her request. It left me with no personal spiritual support. My mom didn't interact with us about religion or God. On Sundays, she dropped us off at the nearest Presbyterian church and picked us up after the service.*
>
> *At age 21, I could no longer buy into some of the religious dogma I had learned as a child. I went metaphysical and started attending the non-denominational Unity Church, which fit me extremely well for forty years. I had a deep relationship with God, but not specifically with Jesus.*

LJ listened intently and then shared about the ancient teachings in the Bible, that I had never read as a young Catholic, or anytime later for that matter. Throughout this conversation, I was crying and my heart felt as if it was going to explode out of my chest. He paused, made sure I was listening, and asked, *"Do you know how much God loves you?"* I said, *"No."*

Then I burst into tears all over again. I sensed the wonder and excitement of what it would feel like to turn my life over to Jesus. Yet at the same time, I was numb, frightened, and mostly quiet, just listening and crying—not really knowing why.

At one point I said, *"You're asking me to give up what I have believed for 40 years."*

"No, I'm asking you to consider accepting Jesus Christ as your Lord and Savior."

"I've been trying all these years to prove that I am a good person and not a sinner, and now you're telling me that I am."

We then looked over some of the Ten Commandments. LJ asked, *"Have you ever dishonored your mother or father?"*

"Yes."

"Have you ever lied?"

"Yes."

"Have you ever stolen?"

"Yes."

"Have you ever cheated?"

"Yes."

"Have you ever murdered?"

"Not physically, however, yes, with my words."

I admitted I was a sinner and continued to feel stirred up in my heart. LJ said there was nothing I had to do right now. When I was ready, all I needed to do was to talk to Jesus, repent, ask for forgiveness, and claim him as my Lord and Savior. I would then receive the Holy Spirit, who from then on, would guide me and direct me to do God's will for my life.

After LJ left, I did just that. I apologized for my humanity as well as my sins and asked Jesus for forgiveness. Then, I acknowledged Him as my Lord and Savior and asked whether he would accept me. Requesting his guidance, I cried myself to sleep and I have not been the same since.

Two days later, I found myself pacing all over my house for about an hour. I called LJ, weeping profusely saying, *"Something is happening to me. I feel energy running up and down my body and it won't stop. It doesn't feel like a panic attack and I don't think I'm having a mental breakdown. My body feels like it's changing from the inside out. I don't know who I am anymore, nothing feels familiar."*

He stayed on the phone with me for quite a while doing his best to calm me down and told me I was receiving the Holy Spirit into my heart, like Jesus promised when I chose to follow Him. I eventually relaxed and felt the presence of God through my body. LJ then told me, *"This is very good news Victoria, you'll be alright. Not everyone has such a profound visceral experience, you are very fortunate."*

As I started reading God's word, many questions came into my mind. After the first week, I asked one of my Christian girlfriends, *"Where in the Bible was there any inspiration? It's all doom and gloom. I'm just about ready to stop reading."*

She asked, *"What part are you reading?"* I told her that I usually start at the end of every book I read.

"Oh Victoria, you're in Revelations, it's at the end for a reason. Start with Matthew in the New Testament that talks about the life of Jesus. You'll find what you are looking for. Keep going."

I did just that and I stayed in touch with LJ to help me understand what I was reading.

As the lockdown restrictions eased, things changed again. I resumed getting physical therapy, acupuncture, and massages in person, which substantially helped maintain my well-being. Happily, I started going out dancing weekly—contra, country, ballroom, west coast swing—I loved every minute if it!

Betsy and I arranged our traditional July birthday dinner at a local restaurant. Her sister joined us—we truly enjoyed being out together, appreciating the fabulous food and each other's company.

Shortly after my birthday, I reached out to Robert to see how he was doing. We had a great conversation, and he offered to come over to look at the usefulness of the cans of paint stored in the laundry room. I took him up on his offer, and after looking at the paint he also repaired the toilet in the apartment bathroom. I hadn't seen him for two years, so it was great catching up with our lives while getting a couple of projects completed.

In late July, I visited my friend Christopher for a week in Pine. It was fun to be out of town again. It was much cooler than Phoenix, so we took some long walks. One evening we went to a small downtown pub and played pool and shuffle board, listened to a local country band, and had a couple of beers.

During the day while he was working, I caught up on my casual reading, which I enjoyed considerably. A special highlight happened Thursday during lunch when we heard some unusual noise outside. We looked out the window and saw a herd of at least ten deer grazing in the yard—I was deeply moved by being connected to nature this way!

Feeling so much more connected to God through Jesus Christ, I now gave Him credit for paving the way for my successes by guiding my every step. I was also honored to be a steward of what I previously thought of as my possessions. I released everything to His care, including my car, home, businesses, health, friendships, and love life.

After finding a new church home and becoming a member, I was led to serve as a greeter on Sunday mornings between services. I was guided to take part in two Bible study groups, one for singles and another for women. The people were accepting of me and fascinated by my testimony.

Never having read God's Word before, I was intrigued by what I was learning. One of my friends asked when I was getting baptized? I told her I was already baptized as an infant in the Catholic faith. She mentioned that the next step as a new adult follower of Jesus, was to publicly die to my old self and declare my new life in Christ Jesus—like a rite of passage. I told her I would consider it. More on this later.

As a new Christian, I actively deepened my relationship with Jesus, which was gladly consuming a lot of my time. Attending my church and Bible study groups was extremely impactful, and I felt truly connected to Jesus. I found myself more focused on other people, instead of putting myself first. As I was no longer drawn to my previous spiritual practices, I stopped going to Unity Church, Equinoxx, Torina, and group meditation sessions. This allowed me to create a new community of like-minded people that I got to know and care about. We socialized when we could and had lots of fun.

Since I was hoping to develop a relationship with a man who had a thirst to know Jesus, I changed my spiritual affiliation on my online dating profile. I thought I might find more compatible matches—WRONG AGAIN! Where were all the good men?

August was a busy month. My neighbor moved all of Bernie's living room furniture out and mine in. Bernie's eldest son took a few pieces, and I sold and donated the rest. After almost two years of clearing, I was ready to make Bernie's home my home—at least for a while. I finally got the last of Bernie's investments transferred into my name—there were twice as many shares as I had expected. How cool is that?

Uh-oh, outside suddenly needed some work—the famous Phoenix monsoons had ripped the siding off the eaves at the front of my house. Luckily, LJ offered to make the repairs—I was happy to have him apply the same skills to my home that he used to maintain his rental properties. He worked on my home several days over the next three months.

In the middle of the month, I made a short and sweet visit to Denver to see friends and family—my first plane trip since I spread Bernie's ashes in 2018.

My friend Karri, who had relocated earlier in the year, picked me up at the airport on Friday. We drove to her place, where I dropped off my bag and changed my shoes. Then we took a long walk through the neighborhood accompanied by her boyfriend and her dog Stiglets.

The next afternoon we went to a local open-air art fair, then out to dinner at one of their favorite restaurants. In the morning, we shopped at the Farmer's Market and followed that up with an outdoor concert. It was wonderful seeing them again.

My cousins Kristin and Jayne picked me up at Karri's on Monday morning and the three of us went shopping—they love shopping. Although, I don't enjoy it as much as they do, walking around appreciating the nice weather and just being together was great. We spent the afternoon playing cards and board games and looking at photo albums of their growing family—it was a really special time. Then they took me to the airport for my evening flight home.

When I got back from Denver, I rented Bernie's room to Paula, while she looked for and bought a condo. One morning Paula walked into the master bathroom—the entire floor was wet. LJ to the rescue again! He came over and found a major plumbing run problem in the kitchen that was causing the leak. It took some ingenuity on his part to fix it, because the pipes were not installed correctly—another item on the *I Should Move List.*

Paula living in my home made getting together for editing my book, *Three Magical Words for a Magical Life,* easy as pie. I had done three retreats at home and attended Tom Bird's virtual workshop earlier in the year to make sure the draft manuscript was ready for Paula's rigorous editing. We worked on it three days a week for two months. Edit, edit, edit—revise, revise, revise. When Paula and I were done editing, Betsy designed the cover and interior layout, as well as formatting the text for the print and eBook. This book was the same genre as the first one, leading Betsy to offer the brilliant idea of creating the *Extraordinary Outcomes Series.*

October 1, I began working again with Denise Cassino every week to prepare my new book for launch in January. She agreed with the *Extraordinary Outcomes Series* idea and said that both books would pop up together on Amazon. Betsy and I then updated both covers. #1 bestseller, here I come again!

The next step in my Christian walk was a public acknowledgment of my new faith in Christ Jesus. On September 24, I was baptized at Christ Church of the Valley. Here's what led up to that special day.

Starting in August, I kept saying to myself, *"I have to get to the water."* I planned to go to San Diego with a new Christian friend, Patty, but we had to cancel the trip due to the California fires. We made a new plan for a day trip to a local lake the following Sunday, as I still needed to get to the water. Patty called that morning and said she couldn't go, so I said, *"I'll go alone, I just have to get to the water."*

Although that day trip was enjoyable, I soon realized that it was the baptismal water I was craving. That's when I knew I was ready to get baptized. On Monday, I made an appointment for Saturday afternoon, September 26. Because I preferred having a small intimate gathering, I only invited Patty and LJ to witness my declaration. I was excited to know that they could attend. The very next day, Deb, my Bible study facilitator, texted me after I told all the women in our Bible study group that I was getting baptized on Saturday. She asked if she could come.

I said, *"You've only met me once over zoom. You don't even know me. Why would you want to come to my baptism?"*

"You are my sister in Christ, I know your heart and your thirst for the Lord."

"How sweet of you. Sure, I'd like that."

Wednesday, my emotions welled-up and I started weeping again—an urgency came over me to be baptized the next day. I called the church weeping and spoke with the receptionist.

"I can't wait until Saturday to be baptized, I need to get into the water as soon as possible."

She replied, *"Do you want to come in today?"*

"No, I have a full day of clients. What time do you open the in morning?"

"8:30, come on over, we'd be glad to witness and celebrate with you."

I contacted LJ, Patty, and Deb to give them the new date. When I arrived, I was shocked to see at least twenty people out on the lawn waiting for me. I guess God's plan was for me to have many supportive witnesses to celebrate with me—it was glorious! I died to my old self and was born again as a new creature in Christ. My heart was overflowing with fulfillment and joy. To my surprise, Patty gave me my first Study Bible and a beautiful cross necklace. I am forever grateful!

On Thanksgiving, I visited my mom in the morning and then went to Linda's for an outdoor potluck. She invited several interesting people I didn't know. We laughed, ate a phenomenal dinner, including homemade pumpkin pie, then had thought-provoking conversations until the evening ended.

On the third anniversary of Bernie's passing. I took a leisurely walk in the park by my house and reflected on the good times we shared. My heart was filled with lots of love! No more pennies—Bernie was off on his spiritual adventure. I continued to feel his presence and kept him close as I moved on—spending time with my friends, working on my books, dancing, clearing out my space, and deepening my relationship with Jesus—creating my fabulous new life.

This Christmas had a completely new meaning for me. In the past, my holidays were focused on getting together with friends and family, sharing wonderful meals, and opening presents. Now, Christmas centered on celebrating the birth of Jesus Christ with the people in my life.

I went to the outdoor service at my church on Christmas Eve with some of my Christian friends, which was especially meaningful to me. Afterward, we took in a movie.

Christmas morning, I picked up my mom and treated her to a sensational brunch at the Marriott Hotel. When we got back to her place, we opened presents and then I went home. That evening, it was time for another movie with some friends.

By the end of the year, I clearly had accomplished most of my 2020 business goals. I added 25 new clients, a 15% increase—thank you for all the referrals Dawn. *Three Magical Words for a Magical Life* was complete for publication in early in 2021. As the spirit moved me, I also continued writing the book you're reading now.

All the clutter was gone, ready to sell, or prepared for pickup, except for his collections of jewelry, minerals, stamps, coins, vinyl records, and art that I needed to have evaluated. Finally, I could completely see the condition of the house, the apartment, and the property—time to weigh the pros and cons of staying or leaving and make a wise choice for myself. As the tremendous fireplace seemed to be the only reason to stay, I was leaning toward selling and buying a home of my own, yet I didn't feel ready.

My walk with God significantly deepened after I accepted Jesus as my Lord and Savior. It transformed my life and filled it with awe and wonder, for which I am so thankful!

What a marvelous year! I ended it with love in my heart for Jesus, for Bernie, and for my incredible life.

The Year of Completion

During 2021, I continued capturing my journey on paper as life moved forward. It took me through a range of emotions from sadness to happiness; frustration to peace; overwhelm to serenity; and everything in-between. Occasionally, as I was writing, beautiful memories of Bernie and I would surface and I'd burst into tears of joy. Other times, it would remind me of his last breath and missing him. I took it all in stride, knowing it was part of my healing.

My mom was much less agitated and began going to group activities, making friends, and settling into the Center as her new home. I felt relieved knowing she was well taken care of. Once again, I was free to focus on my precious life. My priorities were to love myself, listen to my inner guidance, and inspire people to live extraordinary lives.

This year's business goals included publishing my second book, preparing this memoir for publication, and being in service to as many new and existing clients as possible. With the pandemic still affecting everyday life, I worked with my clients by phone. They continued to thrive despite their circumstances and enjoyed their results. I also wrote monthly articles for the Repatterning Practitioner's Association Journal that I took genuine pleasure in doing.

The print and eBook versions of the second book in my Extraordinary Outcomes Series, *Three Magical Words for a Magical Life,* launched the first week in January and reached #1 on Amazon within 24 hours. Yay—what an outstanding way to start the year! I was ecstatic all over again. Just as I had done the first time, I ran outside and jumped up and down. Then I called Betsy, Paula, and Denise to tell them the good news and thank them for all their expertise and hard work. Once more, my adrenaline rush lasted the whole day.

With Bernie's remaining treasures ready for sale, I knew the fall would be a good time to buy a place of my own. As you'll see, God had a different plan.

On January 5, Deb, my Bible study facilitator, came over for a visit. Although the house was no longer overrun with clutter, I was still embarrassed to have a new friend see the condition of my home. I told her I was trying to decide whether to use the money from the sale of my condo to stay and renovate or sell and move on, and that my plan was to choose by the fall. She asked me what I was waiting for. I let her know I had so many things going on—my business, my books, my mom, my relationships, my life. The idea of using my time and energy to look, decide, sell, buy, pack, move, and unpack was just too much to consider. I also wasn't sure what I could afford. Deb is a Realtor and understood my considerations.

She asked, *"Do you have any facts?"*

"No, I don't."

She suggested that gathering information would help me when I got ready to choose. She recommended I get pre-qualified for a loan so I would know what price range I could consider—it would be good to get the facts. The following day, I qualified for a mortgage that would allow me to buy what I knew I wanted, if I could find it—it was good to get the facts. Deb had contacted a contractor who came over to give me a remodeling estimate for Bernie's place to see if it would be worth renovating before selling. He told me I wouldn't get back what I put in if I did that—it was good to get the facts.

Deb set up an MLS listing portal for me, so I could see what was available at my leisure. She told me that if I saw a home I liked, we could go and look at it—no obligation. I thought that it certainly couldn't hurt.

I looked on the MLS and found a charming 1000 sq ft house in a 55+ community on the east side of town, just where I wished to be—perfect. Deb and I went to see the house. I fell in love as soon as I saw it, but I wanted to check out a few more options. We looked at two more places that day, which confirmed the first one was perfect for me. The time and money it would take to fix up Bernie's place was overwhelming, making it a no-brainer to make an offer on this cute little house.

In the exceedingly active Phoenix market, I put in a bid that afternoon and the seller accepted right away—I signed the contract at 5:00 pm. I was thrilled that it had happened so fast. Guess I wasn't waiting for the Autumn leaves.

Time to get the remaining items in the house evaluated to find out what could be sold. My friend Kathryn, who is an estate sale expert, was the perfect person to help me. She went through my entire home figuring out what had value and what didn't—what to sell, what to donate, and what to keep. Then she told me I probably wouldn't net very much money after the agent fee if I had an estate sale. Even though it was a lot more work, I decided a yard sale was the way to go.

I also asked her to look at Bernie's gem, jewelry, and stamp collections and advise me on how to have them appraised for sale and find some buyers. I took photos of part of Bernie's mineral collection, which I texted to Kathryn's contact. Using his quote, I had an idea about the value of the complete collection. She recommended an expert who would evaluate the gold jewelry and suggested people whom I could call about how to get started selling the artwork. She didn't have any contacts available for the coins or stamps—I figured I'd deal with that later. The vinyl was in terrible shape, and I decided it wasn't worth the extra effort to seek out buyers. What a blessing Kathryn was!

When the evaluation, sorting, donating, and releasing of the piles of stuff in the house was complete, I prepared to sell what was left. My first ever yard sale happened at the beginning of February. Paula and I spent two days cleaning, organizing, and pricing everything, except for the furniture. On Friday morning, LJ provided major support by getting it all outside, figuring out where to put things, and how to display them to attract the buyers. We sold a lot of the smaller items on the first day. I also received two inquiries about buying Bernie's house, one from a neighbor and another from a young couple with five children. Cool beans!

Betsy came to help on Saturday and help she did. She was so gregarious and engaged everyone who stopped by, suggesting they buy a certain item and they would—it was amazing. I worked the yard sale alone on the last day—I made $2,500 and there was still plenty of stuff to sell. Some of it I moved inside and left the bigger pieces on my driveway. About a week afterward, I loaded up and donated some items that hadn't sold, and everything still outside went back inside.

A few days later, I walked through Bernie's house with the young couple who had asked about it. They loved the layout and thought the apartment would be perfect for their two teenagers. Besides making an awesome cash offer, $125,000 above the one I received three years ago, they bought my living room end tables—COOL. Not wanting to rush into a decision and planning to research more options, I let them know I wasn't ready to sell just yet. They told me they were not in a hurry and to take my time. Three weeks later, my neighbor's Realtor/investor evaluated my home as a flip and made an offer $20,000 below the couple's bid, which was looking pretty good for them.

Deb, Betsy, and I did a walk-through at the new house on February 21. We measured the rooms and took videos. Betsy used our results and applied her astounding graphic design skills to create a printed layout. This made it easy to visualize the placement of my furniture in each room, including how I could see the mountain view from my office. It looked to be a pretty tight fit, and I started wondering how it all would work for me—the need to downsize was really taking hold. I sold some furniture to accommodate the available space and could hardly wait to close on March 1.

In February, I had asked the mortgage broker if using cash for the down payment would be a problem. He told me it wouldn't. Later on it was apparent that the documentation for the cash was paper thin, so securing the mortgage became an issue. This got vastly more complicated when a friend tried to help me solve it.

The morning I was supposed to close, I received a phone call from the broker informing me that my loan wasn't approved and I had lost the house. I thought he was kidding, but he wasn't—I was crushed! My dream and all my plans vanished in the blink of an eye. I was angry and sad. After the shock wore off, I called the broker to ask if there was anything we could do, like more money down, to qualify for a smaller mortgage. The answer was no!

Then I got a call from Deb. She was shocked that the financing hadn't gone through and upset that the broker didn't keep her informed about the situation. She also told me that on top of losing the house, I lost my earnest money due to bad timing on her part. I just about came unglued. She acknowledged it was her mistake and she would repay me personally. Now that's integrity!

It was a couple of days before I could even pick up the phone to get the support I needed from my friends. I was also angry at God, who promised me the purchase would go through. He let me know that his plans for me had changed and something better was on its way. I asked Him, *"Why didn't you warn me? Did you have to wait till the last minute? This is devastating!"* It took me about a week to calm down and restore my trust in God again.

I needed a break from house hunting, which I gladly gave myself. In mid-March, another investor called me, came over, and offered me $15,000 more than the young couple's bid. I let him know that my preference was to have the young couple buy it because they wanted to renovate and live there, and I hoped to pass the baton from Bernie to their family. Naturally, he was disappointed. Now, I had all the figures I needed to present the couple with my final counter-offer—they accepted. Yay!

I had taken a month off to recover from not getting the mortgage and started looking again. After house hunting with Deb ten times over three weeks viewing twenty-five houses, I almost gave up. It was a seller's market. People were offering thousands over the asking price, site unseen. Increasing my top offer would leave me with a larger mortgage—I simply could not compete. Guess I would have to wait until September after all—BOO.

I advertised my *Free-for-the-Taking Day* at the end of March to get rid of what hadn't been sold. My friend Terry was a tremendous help. By 6:00 in the morning, he had single-handedly moved all of Bernie's bedroom furniture outside, which included a dresser, nightstands, and his California king waterbed frame, plus several bookcases, four desks, and the yard sale leftovers. The box springs and mattress went out for bulk trash. Wow! Whatever wasn't taken then was put out on the curb and eventually someone picked it up.

Watching the TV series *The Chosen,* that portrays Jesus through the eyes of those who met him, made the Bible come alive for me. Every week, I digested another episode and began integrating Christian principles into my life. Every day in every way I felt changed somehow from the inside out.

Holy Week had a significant meaning for me this year. I was very contemplative during this time. Getting in touch with Jesus' suffering for my benefit during the Good Friday service at my church, I knew I was sanctified and blessed. Easter Sunday, which I now refer to as Resurrection Sunday, was more meaningful than it ever had been. It signified the promises God made that were now available to me. I had a quiet day to myself. After church, I took a long bike ride in the park and that evening, I watched another episode of *The Chosen.* Holy Week felt very inspirational and sacred.

On April 30, I closed on the cash sale of Bernie's house. The buyers let me know I could stay until the end of July—three months rent free, LUCKY ME! I took full advantage of their generosity—following my heart without regret! By May 3, the cash from the sale of Bernie's house was in the bank—so I now had well-documented money to use to purchase a new home.

I mustered the courage to look on the MLS again. It surprised me to find a townhouse in the same area as the one that had fallen through. Deb and I went to see it the next day—I fell in love once more. It was even better than the first place. Just maybe, God was looking out for me. To increase my chances of buying this house, I instantly made an AS-IS-no-contingencies offer. After a bit of a bidding war, I won by going 8% over the asking price, which took most of my savings. I trusted things would work out and I would be taken care of. Friday was the inspection—I was good to go. Unbelievable, from finding it to offer acceptance in four days!

I closed on my new home on June 18, picked up the keys, performed a house blessing the next day, and claimed it as my own! God was right, this townhouse was a much better place for me. It was 1250 sq ft with an open layout. Every room had been totally renovated. Everything was new—the kitchen; all the appliances; fixtures in both bathrooms; flooring and lighting throughout; as well as the Arizona room's natural wood paneling.

Flowering bushes and beautiful plants filled the small front yard, and I could see a slice of Lookout Mountain from the porch. The Arizona room provided a view onto my modest backyard with a wonderful shade tree and four blooming vines sprawling the length of the wall. It felt like I was going from a dungeon to the Taj Mahal!

There were a few things I planned to change to make the cabinets and closet spaces more useful. I was desperately in need of more shelving. Robert was my best resource, so I contacted him and went over to his house—it was delightful to see him again. He said he missed our friendship and was glad I reached out. We enjoyed discussing the modifications to be made and getting caught up.

I had four weeks left to release whatever I wasn't taking, pack up what I was keeping, and move. Each week, a few of my friends helped me pack several boxes, which we took to my new house and unpacked. This way, I could get settled in before moving day. Just when I thought I was done, I suddenly remembered Bernie's attic crawl space—oh no! I was so leery of going up there. I was sure it would be packed to the rafters with more stuff. Fortunately, there were only a few Christmas decorations I had never seen, which I swiftly donated.

Betsy spent several days helping me clear out and clean up Bernie's master suite. Then we moved all of my clothes out of his closet into mine. Now, his area was empty and my closet was jam-packed. I could barely get anything out—it motivated me to go through it and donate what I no longer wanted.

Books, books, books—books in the living room and every room of the apartment. Betsy and I sorted and packed hundreds of books from the bookcases that were stuffed to the gills. In the end, we had 57 boxes, including 20 boxes that had been stored for over 10 years. I donated everything to Arizona Book Donations. They sort and distribute books by category to organizations throughout the Phoenix metropolitan area.

Bernie's stamp collection needed to be evaluated—the philatelist told me it contained nothing of value. I kept the U.S. stamps that were not canceled, then gave the rest to the Boys and Girls Club—they were so appreciative.

Remember the hot tub? When I couldn't find anyone who wanted it, Christopher came to the rescue—just in time for bulk trash day. He rented a reciprocating saw and chopped it into several pieces, then my neighbor helped to drag each section to the curb. When they finished, I served them both a well-deserved meal—what a weight out of my space and off my mind.

Time to plan my move. Phoenix in the summer is extremely HOT, so I didn't want my friends hauling heavy stuff in the heat—I wanted to keep them as friends. Since I had spent most of my emergency money buying the house, I had little to spend on moving. I started calling movers—yikes, $1000 was the lowest quote I got. Happily, miracles happened, and I had a full crew by 6:00 in the morning on moving day—five men, four trucks, one van, and a trailer.

When I first decided to move, LJ offered to bring his van and trailer. On July 4, I went to a party at my friend Nan's. Her daughter's boyfriend, Matt, said he'd heard that I was moving and asked if I needed any help. My mouth opened and the word YES jumped out. Bryan, who I met at Linda's, called me two days before the move and asked what I was up to. When I told him, he said he would help. My neighbor, Kyle, who was also getting ready to move, let me know he was available on moving day.

We began bright and early on July 17. Matt, Bryan, Kyle, and LJ all showed up with their trucks and trailers—we got started. As we completed loading up the vehicles, my neighbors, Mike and Gladys, brought their truck over and filled it with all my plants. Just as I hoped, we only had to make one trip. A couple of my girlfriends came over after we were done, and we unpacked most of the boxes.

I couldn't have asked for the move to go any better—it was amazing! Who offers to help anyone move these days? I considered myself so blessed!

Four days after moving, I began working with clients over the phone. It only took ten days for Robert and I to organize my new home, so I had a place for everything and everything was in its place. It was wonderful—I could find anything I needed whenever I needed it. I had created a firm foundation for myself from which I could catapult forward in my life. What a feeling!

I was excited to bring my mom to my new home—she told me it was beautiful and she was proud of me. We began having FaceTime sessions with my brother and sisters—she really loved being able to see them, talk about how things were going for them, and ask when they were coming to visit.

Whenever I took mom back to the Center, she became exceedingly agitated and had a hard time reorienting to her room. It broke my heart—I didn't know how to deal with her frustration other than letting her know she was well taken care of and safe. She needed me to stay for a good hour before she was comfortable enough for me to leave. I realized that taking her to my place just didn't work for her well-being, so excursions stopped and instead I visited her at the Center weekly.

She was becoming more aware of how her mind was deteriorating, and she kept saying, *"There's something wrong with my brain. I'm not sure if I'm doing everything I'm supposed to be doing."* I assured her that there was nothing she could do wrong and that a nursing assistant would come to get her if she wasn't on time to eat. It was hard for her to believe that they would do that. To ease her mind, I told her I thought research was being done to develop medicine to help her and hopefully find a cure. I reminded her that the nurses on staff were there if she needed anything or wanted to call me—they were doing their best to keep her safe and comfortable.

In order to sell off the few remaining things at Bernie's, I posted specific listings on Offer-Up and Craig's List, including another yard sale. I sold most of the furniture, along with the firepit, the patio set, a vacuum cleaner, some lamps, and items left from my previous yard sale—everything else went to the curb. Although I made some money when I released Bernie's treasures, I'm sure his ashes jumped out of the ocean every time I missed an opportunity to make more money. To me, the time and effort it would take to evaluate, clean, price, advertise, and sell those used items—which *might* bring in a little bit of cash—was over the top. I threw away at least half, donated what could be useful to others, took in about $5,000 on what I sold, and found $3,000 around the house, including some Euros in one of the file cabinets. Cha-Ching!

It took me three and half years—a 3-ton dumpster; 12 bulk trash pickups; 2 yard sales; Offer-Up and Craigslist ads; a *Free-for-the-Taking Day;* and innumerable runs to Goodwill, Salvation Army, and St. Vincent de Paul to liberate myself from Bernie's treasures. I'm certain Bernie's stuff made many families happy. Finally, all of Bernie's treasures were released and removed, although I still had his mineral, jewelry, artwork, and coin collections to be sold later. I deeply appreciate all the incredible people who gave selflessly of their time and energy to make sure the clear-out was accomplished! Thank you so much to all those who helped me. I couldn't have done it without you. I am so fortunate to have all of you in my life.

At the beginning of the year, I had no idea I'd be finishing up with releasing Bernie's clutter, selling his house, and buying a fabulous townhouse in a neighborhood I loved. Bernie was right—no matter where I was, I took him with me, and I didn't need to stay in his house to do so. Selling Bernie's place for top dollar enabled me to buy the perfect, right-sized, home for me.

By July 31, it was time to pass the baton to the new homeowner to enjoy with their five children. It felt so good to honor Bernie by handing his keys to the new owners and close this chapter of my life. Now, I was free to embrace my new life in my new home with satisfaction and gusto—I haven't looked back since. What an fascinating journey of self-discovery and personal resolve!

Thank God for Robert. He was instrumental in assisting me with many projects in my townhouse that needed attention. He stayed for a couple of weeks in my second bedroom. We resumed our many hours of deep, rich conversations, and caught up on what had happened in our lives over the past few years. Our friendship was deepening and expanding for sure.

At first, I hesitated to pursue anything beyond companionship, because I wanted to honor Robert's desire to continue his spiritual pursuits. He had previously told me that being in a relationship would distract him. Truth be told, he admitted that after Bernie died, he was scared to death to engage in an intimate relationship with me. Robert explained that he'd been divorced for fifteen years and had never even considered another relationship.

To my surprise one evening, while Robert and I were watching a movie, Bernie's best friend leaned over and kissed me.

We both asked, *"What's going on?"*

He said, *"I kinda sorta like you a little."*

I gave him a big smile, *"I kinda sorta like you a little, too."*

He let me know he had completed his spiritual pursuits as far as he could go and was open to what life would offer next.

After Robert went back home, we got together every week—I'd make dinner, we'd watch a movie, and cuddle and kiss, although there was no commitment to exclusivity we enjoyed each other's company. It was way too early to determine where we were headed—all I knew was that I was happy and our friendship felt very comfortable and intimate.

Before our budding romance started, I had been wanting to find a Christian man who danced—Robert was neither.

In mid-September, I was dancing at the Arizona American Italian Club—

where they had a live band every Friday and Saturday night. While my friend Joe and I were taking a break and talking about relationships, I told him I was looking for a Christian man. He said he thought Karl, whom I had danced with that evening, was a Christian. As I was leaving, I approached Karl and thanked him for the dances.

While I was dancing with Karl the following Saturday, he asked me out, and I said yes. A few days later, we had a wonderful time at a local karaoke bar, listening and dancing between the tables. During our conversation, he confirmed he was a Christian, and I shared my testimony as a new follower of Christ. He then told me about the home fellowship he attended and invited me to come on Sunday, which I did. The pastor presented verses from scripture connected to a specific principle. We followed along and asked questions at the end—I could relate these passages to me personally. I started attending this fellowship before church on Sundays. Being new to the Bible, it helped me integrate the biblical principles I was learning into my life.

The day after I attended my first fellowship service with Karl, Robert and I took off to Breezy Pines for a week-long, off-the-grid break from working on projects around my house.

Before I left town, I sent the manuscript for this book to Paula for her estimate of the work we would need to do. I had not been out of town for a year and was overdue for a vacation. Robert and Bernie had spent a lot of time with their respective children at the cabin over the years. Being there brought back wonderful memories for both of us.

I got unpacked and relaxed while Robert took care of making sure the utilities were turned on. We went hiking up in the hills and collected large, colorful stones for my yard. It reminded me of the rock collection I had as a little girl. We made great tasting, healthy meals and watched movies—we were so comfortable with each other. I read one of my yet-to-be-published books about the Fairy Realm to him, which he thoroughly enjoyed.

It was 47° at night, a good excuse to just sit in front of a roaring fire and cuddle to stay warm. Kisses galore!

After our trip to Breezy Pines and a couple of more dates with Karl, I realized I had in Robert a deep love and friendship that was undeniable. I just couldn't, nor did I want to, split my affection—I don't know how women date more than one guy at a time.

I stopped dating Karl, and he took me under his wing as my Bible mentor. We met every week for twelve weeks, after the home fellowship service, to watch a video series on how to interpret the Bible. This specific study substantially improved my understanding and it was beginning to make sense. I also saw Robert a few times a week—this worked for all three of us.

Because Robert and I had so much going for us, my previous desire to date a Christian man who danced, was fading away. We were encouraging and respectful of each other's spiritual journey, and he agreed to take dance lessons. We discovered at his first lesson that Robert had two, maybe three, left feet and decided dancing wasn't for him. Bernie was not a dancer either and I got used to going without him, so I knew I could do it again.

Robert and I spent a lovely Autumn in rich conversations, cooking delightful meals, watching movies at home, hiking on South and Lookout Mountains, all while decorating my townhouse. We also had a blast kayaking on Bartlett Lake—he only brought one paddle. I felt like a princess being floated around by my loyal knight!

As Robert and I were getting closer, I started to feel uncomfortable with all the ways he was supporting me. I wasn't used to a man wanting to engage so deeply with me as well as make my life easier. He often served me coffee in the morning; packed my lunch when I was working away from home; kept my car in tip-top condition; cleaned my house; along with many other acts of kindness—incredible!

His attention to my needs allowed me to focus on my clients, my books, my friends, and my dancing. We talked about my discomfort, and he told me, *"It's time to get used to different."* I surrendered to his way of expressing and showing his love for me—allowing his support to become natural to me.

Thanksgiving was lovely. Robert and I visited my mom, played cards, looked through the family photo albums, and FaceTimed with my siblings. She was happy after talking with them—it was a perfect way to celebrate with family. Afterward, we went to Michael and Patti's annual Thanksgiving gathering—Robert got along famously with my friends.

Christmas day this year was especially meaningful to me. In the morning, Robert and I again visited my mom, bearing gifts to and from her. She expressed how grateful she was for me and my time this year. We played cards, and she won five of the six games. Go, mom, go!

For the first time in fourteen years, I hosted a holiday celebration in my home—Christmas dinner for six felt just right. Robert and I had fun preparing the menu and cooking the main dishes—baked ham, garlic mashed potatoes, Brussels sprouts with sesame seeds, and homemade spelt-crust pumpkin pie. Our guests each brought a dish to add to the feast—and a feast it was! We all thoroughly enjoyed the meal and each other's company especially our in-depth conversations that covered a variety of interesting topics. I was proud of my new home and delighted to have people I cared about over to celebrate with me.

During the following week, I reviewed the business goals I had set for the year. My most significant accomplishment was publishing my second book, which reached #1 on Amazon in one day. I joined an online marketing platform called AllAuthors, that increased my exposure and ability to promote my books through weekly Twitter posts designed to attract readers. By the end of the year, sales had grown. Yay! I also finished writing this book. Paula and I were meeting at her house twice a week to, you guessed it—edit, edit, edit, revise, revise, revise. I was enthusiastic about completing the work to have it ready for publication before the end of 2022.

New Year's Eve was another chance to celebrate life, which I did by creating a festive, peaceful, and loving evening with Robert. As it often did, our conversation became deeply personal. This time, I shared about how I had approached the holiday season before I met Bernie.

Early in December each year, I would evaluate my current romantic relationship. If it wasn't working for me, I'd think, if I start the new year with this man, I'll have the same year I had last year. It didn't make sense to me to share holiday time, visit relatives, and exchange gifts with someone I was no longer interested in dating. It felt disrespectful, so I would release the relationship. The problem with doing this was that I often spent my holidays alone and felt like a third wheel when I was with my friends who were partnered up.

I let Robert know this Christmas had been so very special to me, with him by my side—I was happy! He gave me a big smile and acknowledged the courage it took for me to share this pattern of behavior at that depth. He later told me that his smile matched his inner happiness and well-being.

Robert and I had developed a new and amazing relationship. The right guy had been right in front of me the whole time—all I had to do was look. I knew deep within my heart that Bernie was jumping for joy! He sent the perfect man for me, after all!

Epilogue

This memoir started with one love story—I had no idea it would end with another.

I am living a full and fabulous life.

I am surrounded by people I cherish, who love and accept me for who I am. My walk with God continues to deepen, through reading His Word daily and attending worship services, as well as Bible study weekly. Riding my bike, taking long walks in the neighborhood, and hiking nearby mountain trails provide me with exercise and a chance to appreciate nature. Eating healthy food, getting massages, facials, and acupuncture treatments maintain my health and well-being.

I gather as much support as I need and give myself time to relax and rejuvenate. Dancing, singing at the Higher Vibrations choir, and going to dinner and the movies with my friends all promote my self-expression. I take fun day trips and vacations to get away from everyday concerns. There is a nice balance between love, work, and play for me. The things I know will feed my soul and rest my mind—I do.

I am making a real and lasting difference.

I found it was so important to be gentle with myself through Bernie's illness, death, and my grieving. I was also kind and patient while settling his estate, cleaning out the house, and moving into a new place. I did my best, knowing that my best was enough.

I am consistently filled with the Holy Spirit and centered in my heart, making it easier to treat people lovingly with consideration and kindness. A significant change I've noticed is that I now focus on those around me rather than on myself and my needs. I seek divine guidance and ask where and how I can make a difference in the lives of others and am given many opportunities for which I am deeply grateful.

The positive changes in my life are too numerous to mention—so many of my prayers have been answered. One that stands out the most is finding a townhouse I loved, having my offer accepted, and the inspection all completed within four days! I'm secure knowing that I have God as my companion guiding me every step of the way and that He loves me profoundly.

I am inspiring and empowering others.

I thoroughly enjoy the office I created in my new home. It's welcoming and comfortable, setting the stage for deep transformational results. Even after thirty years, I still love the work I do with my clients. It gives me an avenue to apply my education, my profound listening skills, my compassion, and my intuitive gifts. When they tell me about the difference working with me has made in their life, I'm always inspired—there's nothing quite like that moment. I am honored to have clients who trust me with their precious lives.

I'm now preparing the third book in my *Extraordinary Outcomes Series*—intended for publication in 2025. It's going to be another valuable one! The act of writing provides me with the opportunity for reflection, allowing my insights to flow onto the page. As I freely express my thoughts, it seems as if each book writes itself—amazing. My ultimate goal is to reach more people in fulfillment of my mission— to inspire and empower myself and others to live extraordinary lives overflowing with love, adventure, passion, and joy!

I am more accepting of the cycles of life.

My mother has acclimated to her environment and is well settled in the assisted living facility. Even though her dementia is now considered severe, she still recognizes me. Once in a while, she gets scared because she isn't sure what she's supposed to do next, or where to go. To reassure her, I remind her that the staff takes good care of her, and I'll be back to visit again. I encourage her to take walks, look through her magazines, attend the various group activities at the Center, and engage with the other residents. There are a few residents there who she likes and talks with, for which I am truly thankful.

My weekly visits with her are meaningful and enjoyable, more so because Robert contributes by being supportive and adds to the quality of her life. We often play her favorite card game, Kings in the Corner, which she frequently wins—with just a few nudges from us. Sometimes we decide to watch a movie or just sit outside and enjoy nature. It's been emotionally difficult seeing my mom lose her capacity to be independent and vital, to even understand the world around her. I'm coming to terms with it more and more every day and am glad to be there for her. I love you, mom.

I am delighting in another love story.

Best of all, Robert is now my partner in living an extraordinary life. Bernie told me three times not to wait too long—he would send the perfect man for me. It took a while, but after a few false starts when I was ready—there he was right in front of me!

Recently, Robert expressed his gratitude that he was honored to be the *"poor sucker"* helping to clean up Bernie's mess. It had given him the chance to nurture his friendship with me. I admire him as a partner because of the character traits he embodies. He's very organized, financially secure, generous in sharing what he has, and has a thirst for knowledge that we share. He wants me by his side, whether we are traveling, out with friends, or simply enjoying our time at home—we have exceptional times, no matter what we're doing. He shares his heart openly, communicates his needs, and listens to mine. The most important quality to me is our spiritual connection and the acceptance of our individual paths. On my birthday in 2023, he asked for my hand in marriage and I whole-heartedly said, YES!

I am eternally grateful.

I'm so grateful for the grand love Bernie and I shared. We had a miraculous relationship. OK...you're right...not always perfect, however, it was 99%...well maybe 98%...uh, realistically 95%...but that's as low as I'll go—in the end love won. Loving him taught me a lot and gave me many occasions to accept him the way he was and the way he wasn't. If I had let his hoarding and financial situation stop me, I would have missed out on ten years of the most magnificent love I have ever experienced. The key for me was to BE all the qualities I wanted to experience—I was often successful and sometimes not so much.

The hours, days, weeks, months, and years, since the day of Bernie's liberation have been filled with many emotions—joy for his liberation, sadness, grief, fear, and anger, as well as delight, optimism, and discovery. Mostly, I let him move on in his journey to his next adventure without always needing to pull him back to me because of my longing to reconnect with him. I can't say I never did this, but it was rare. It was an honor and a privilege to love him and be loved by him. I am eternally grateful!

My everyday life is filled with the joy of my relationships with God, Robert, my mom, and my many friends and colleagues. I am extremely excited to live into my new future, that began with knowing—there is *No Weeping Widow Here!*

Acknowledgments

This book was made possible with the unwavering support of the following wonderful people who helped during the many phases of its birth. I begin by acknowledging myself for listening to my nudge to write, and for my courage, dedication, and perseverance along the way. I am grateful to Tom Bird, the book whisperer, who taught me how to write from my heart, (tombird.com).

I honor the following experts with the deepest gratitude humanly possible—Paula Hofmeister, Betsy McGrew, and Denise Cassino. Thank you to Paula, my extraordinary wordsmith whose unending attention to style and editing detail is off the charts. My heartfelt recognition to Betsy McGrew, my award-winning graphic designer, for her intuitive vision and relentless dedication to formatting this book, along with designing its beautiful cover and updating my fabulous website. Much appreciation to Denise Cassino, (bestsellerservices.com), for once again providing immeasurable assistance in promoting this memoir. You're the best!

The invaluable insights provided by my beta readers: Patti, Connie, Robert, Betsy, and Millie, allowed me to put the perfect finishing touches on my story—thank you all from the bottom of my heart.

So dear to me are my sweetheart Robert and Bernie's friend Christopher, two special men who lent a helping hand to Bernie during his health challenge. Your love and devotion will always be remembered.

Thank you, Dr. Jacobsen, for your expertise and care; Dave Sharma and David Banks for acquiring Bernie's prostheses, which gave him the ability to walk again; and hospice nurse Mikelle Swafford, whose service was tremendous in preserving Bernie's dignity and comfort until the end.

Bless your heart Linda, for opening your beautiful home for the *Celebrate Life with Bernie* event; my endless appreciation to Jim the Gong Master whose

Tibetan sound healing touched Bernie's soul; and to the many, many people who attended. You made it possible for Bernie to know the huge difference he made in your lives and in the world around him.

There will always be a special bond with Reverend Tina, Hans, and Bernie's oldest son, who were present as Bernie liberated his soul from his physical body. Thank you to Bernie's family in Germany and in Phoenix for accepting and including me.

A warm hug goes out to my friends who provided our last Thanksgiving meal together—it was incredibly memorable. Also, to Rudrani and Donna, who traveled from New Mexico to comfort me after Bernie passed. Your presence will always be special to me.

Special appreciation goes to Ron, Bernie's supervisor, who set up the Go Fund Me account that helped with Bernie's medical expenses, and to the 65 generous contributors! You rock! Also, Kenneth, Bernie's HR manager, and Gene, who made it possible for me to fulfill Bernie's wish to have his ashes spread in the ocean from the beach on Kauai.

Gold medals go to Hans, Paula, Mimi, Angela, Kathryn, Christopher, Betsy, LJ, Terry, and especially Robert. They gave selflessly of their time to help clear Bernie's clutter, so I could claim his home as mine, giving me the space to renovate or move. I chose to move—it was the perfect answer.

Thanks to Deb, my realtor, who helped me purchase my new home and the generous people who helped me move in the heat of the summer; Matt, Kyle, LJ, Bryan, Mike, and Gladys. I am forever grateful!

Appreciation to all my dear friends: the Higher Vibrations choir, my new Christian family, and the Fab Five—all of whom have been at my side every step of the way.

I am who, and where I am today, because of the love of my mother, late father, and siblings—all silent supporters of my many adventures, although often beyond their realm of conventional thinking, they support me just the same. Thanks to my siblings for traveling to Arizona to help settle our mom's estate and to Jerry, who completed the process we started.

Last but not least, I extend profound appreciation to my biggest fan, my late beloved husband, Bernie, whose unconditional love for me and outstanding support for my greatness has been a solid foundation from which I continue to discover and explore the writer within.

Bernie, thanks for sending me Robert, who was right in front of me the whole time. Please know that Robert's love for me and my love for him is an extention of the neverending love I shared with you.

About the Author

I'm Victoria Benoit, Mind/Body Repatterning™ expert and Amazon #1 Bestselling Author and Publisher—residing in Phoenix, Arizona. I am a fun-loving, optimistic woman living an extraordinarily rich life, filled with passion, love, and adventure. Along with writing, speaking, and facilitating transformational healing, I enjoy Ballroom, Country, and West Coast Swing dancing; singing; biking; hiking; spending time in nature; and traveling to beaches around the world. My friends and family are especially dear to me, no matter what we're doing. My biggest fan was my Beloved Bernie of ten years, who liberated his soul from his physical body on November 27, 2017.

I grew up in Milwaukee, WI, with my younger brother and two sisters. At 20 years old, I seized an opportunity to move to the big city of Chicago—knowing no one—relying solely on my own sense of adventure. The next 16 years were both routine and eventful. While having a successful career in medical ultrasound and being married and divorced, I began my journey of personal growth and transformation.

In 1989, I decided it was time to move on from the Windy City to Phoenix, the Valley of the Sun. Shortly after moving, I was forced to change careers due to a physical injury at work. In examining what to do next, I saw that through my work as a neonatal ultrasound technician, I had experienced my natural ability to provide a space of profound love and compassion for couples in the initial stage of grief over the loss of their baby. I applied this insight to create a new career in supporting people through tough times.

The next step in my journey was to obtain my master's degree and begin working as a Licensed Professional Counselor. I was quickly frustrated by my clients' lack of progress using traditional methodologies. I decided to study other approaches to support people in creating lives they loved. This guided me to become a Certified Repatterning Practitioner and Teacher. I then began working part time with private clients, using this process to identify and clear their unconscious patterns. Session after session, they reported experiencing extraordinary outcomes in their lives.

Based on my results with private clients, I left traditional counseling completely in 1996, and opened the *Center for Extraordinary Outcomes*. Along with seeing clients, I taught Resonance Repatterning® domestically and internationally for fifteen years, developed workshops, and continued to study and implement additional holistic healing therapies in my practice. Over the years, it became apparent that I needed to stop teaching and start writing to fulfill my desire to impact even more people.

In addition to the book you're reading, I've published two books which swiftly reached #1 on Amazon: *What Would Love Do Right Now? A Guide to Living an Extraordinary Life* in December 2017, and *Three Magical Words for a Magical Life* in January 2021. Through these books, I believe I am making a positive influence on a more global scale.

I absolutely love the difference I make in the world. I am committed to helping people live a life they love—one that is overflowing with love, joy, passion, and fulfillment!

About Extraordinary Outcomes Series
Book One

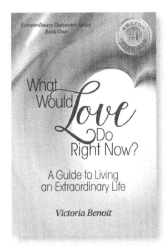

Living from your heart is possible! Asking yourself, *"What would love do right now?"* can be as impactful to your life as Jack Canfield's Chicken Soup is to his readers' souls.

In this step-by-step guide to living an extraordinary life, Victoria shares her philosophy about the power of love, forgiveness, making amends, and emotional healing in those areas and relationships that effect your quality of life today—family, career, romance, health, finances, and self-expression. You will be able to release and heal the pain and suffering from past heartaches, disappointments, and failures that undermine your ability to manifest your dreams and prevent you from living the life you were born to live.

Extraordinary lives are filled with adventures that have a beginning, middle and end; however, asking the question, *"What would love do right now?"* is always useful at any time, in any place, and with anyone—forever.

ExtraordinaryOutcomesPublishing.com/what-would-love-do-right-now/
Amazon.com/What-Would-Love-Right-Extraordinary/dp/0983856702/

About Extraordinary Outcomes Series Book Two

Living a magical life is possible! This book is about you and your life. It's designed for you to use three magical words to free yourself from past hurts that you have received and caused. If your past is unresolved, it not only impacts your life today, it impacts your future. Your old thoughts and patterns will continue to show up in your life until you heal them. How can you create a magical life if your past is interfering? Using a four-step process, you will take an inner journey into some unhealed territory, but the rewards will be worth it—I promise. Starting with your parents and your intimate partners, then your children and siblings, followed by your extended family, next your friends, teachers, coaches, clergy, etc.—and finally, your work associates.

After you have completed the healing, you now have a clean slate to design your magical life filled with love, adventure, creativity, passion, and joy. It starts with *Three Magical Words* and ends with *A Magical Life!*

ExtraordinaryOutcomesPublishing.com/three-magical-words-for-a-magical-life/

Amazon.com/Three-Magical-Words-Life/dp/0983856729/

Stay Connected

Thank you for purchasing this book. I trust you enjoyed it.
To inspire others, please write a review about this book and share an
extraordinary outcome that made a difference in your life
on Amazon.com, Goodreads.com, and/or
ExtraordinaryOutcomesPublishing.com.

Be the first to hear about my new releases and bargains.
Sign up at the link provided below to be on the VIP list.

I promise not to share your email with anyone or clutter your inbox.
ExtraordinaryOutcomesPublishing.com/stay-connected/

For more information about my transformational healing work, visit my
website at: ExtraordinaryOutcomes.com/

Made in the USA
Monee, IL
20 November 2023

46905982R00125